Media/Classroom Skills:
Games for the Middle School
Volume 1

Related titles by the authors of
Media/Classroom Skills: Games for the Middle School, Volume 1

- *Basic Media Skills through Games*

- *Basic Classroom Skills through Games*

- *Media/Classroom Skills: Games for the Middle School, Volume 2*

Media/Classroom Skills
Games for the Middle School
Volume 1

Jeanne E. Wieckert	Irene Wood Bell
Media Specialist	Media Specialist
Denver Public Schools	Denver Public Schools

Illustrated by
Jay Conley

Libraries Unlimited, Inc.
Littleton, Colorado
1981

LIBRARIES UNLIMITED, INC.
P.O. Box 263
Littleton, Colorado 80160

Library of Congress Cataloging in Publication Data

Wieckert, Jeanne E., 1939-
    Media/classroom skills.

    Includes indexes.
    1. Educational games--Handbooks, manuals, etc.
2. Middle schools--United States--Curricula--Hand-
books, manuals, etc. 3. Instructional materials
centers--Handbooks, manuals, etc. I. Bell, Irene
Wood, 1944-   . II. Title.
LB1029.G3W49   373.13   81-2304
ISBN 0-87287-254-8 (set)   AACR2
ISBN 0-87287-227-0 (v. 1)

Libraries Unlimited books are bound with Type II nonwoven material that meets
and exceeds National Association of State Textbook Administrators' Type II
nonwoven material specifications Class A through E.

To Dr. Roy Krosky who removed the "rocks in the road" for me.

—J.E.W.

FOREWORD

More than 90 games are presented in *Media/Classroom Skills: Games for the Middle Schools, Vol. 1*. The games have developed as an extension of the teaching methods embodied in *Basic Media Skills through Games* (Libraries Unlimited, 1979) and *Basic Classroom Skills through Games* (Libraries Unlimited, 1980). They are intended to aid in the introduction, reinforcement, and review of learning skills used in the curriculum areas of the media center, language arts, social studies, foreign languages, and art. (More games dealing in other curriculum areas are to be included in a companion volume, *Media/Classroom Skills: Games for the Middle School, Vol. 2*.) The purpose of these games is twofold: to provide motivation for student involvement and to serve as a means of involving teachers from *all* subject areas in the use of the IMC (Instructional Media Center).

To utilize *Media/Classroom Skills: Games for the Middle Schools, Vol. 1* effectively, the variety of types of games and their adaptability to a wide range of situations need to be considered. Some materials can be prepared for classroom check-out, while other materials can be prepared for use in the media center. For example, "Lango" and "Pyramid Probe," both language arts games, are clearly games that can be utilized in the classroom. "Celebrities" and "Portrait Puzzlers" are both art games that require the use of reference materials found in the media center. Ideally, games will be produced cooperatively by teachers and the media specialist with additions, variations, and refinements to fit individual requirements and philosophies. Each game can be adapted to a particular grade level or skill by substituting a different set of questions or a different list. The foreign language games, for instance, focus upon Spanish and French as the languages most commonly introduced in the middle school, but all of the games in this section are readily adaptable to other languages. A game may be utilized as a team effort or as an individual activity, depending on the needs of a given group. The combinations and adaptations of these games allow the media specialist and teachers to approach skills in all areas of the curriculum. All games make use of inexpensive materials that are readily available in most schools, and once a game is constructed, it can be used repeatedly.

The six sections of the book include an introductory chapter and five chapters of games designed for use in particular subject areas. Three tests are included in the introductory chapter for use as pre-tests and post-tests for media skills. These tests are not standardized and are intended to identify areas in which students need additional help and to indicate mastery of skills. They are intended to be used as guides, as are the "Steps for Construction of Games." Also included in the introductory chapter are the career game, "Pinnacle Point," and career lists for the media specialist to use as initial materials for promoting the use of games with students and teachers. One board can be made with a set of cards pertaining to each career area. Using the same board, the correct set of cards can be substituted to explore a particular career area.

The explanation of the purpose of each game is included in the table of contents to aid the teacher in choosing those games that will be most adaptable to his or her situation and needs. The asterisks in the table of contents are used to indicate those games that take little or no preparation on the part of the teachers and media specialists. These games offer a means for teachers to inaugurate this approach, while other games are being prepared. In addition to the index of game titles a series of selection indexes has been included to permit selection by game type and method of checking and to aid teachers and media specialists in locating those games that will best suit the limitations of class size and time period.

As discussed in the section "New Approaches in Media Instruction," the elements of competition and cooperation have been found to be very effective in transmitting and reinforcing skills, and for this reason, games are structured so that winners (teams or individuals) can emerge, which always adds an air of interest for students. Teachers or media specialists can decide whether or not actual prizes will be awarded; some teachers may wish to use points to help determine grades. All games require students to check or evaluate themselves or each other (with the teacher or media specialist as arbiter).

Lists of materials and instructions for each game are complete and self-contained. Setting some guidelines prior to using the games will possibly prevent confusion, inconvenience, or destruction of materials. First, the game to be used should be read thoroughly by the teacher or media specialist far enough in advance that there will be time to make the materials—some will require a few hours to prepare. Also, keeping the book (or a copy of the game rules) handy during play will help if consultation of the rules in some of the more complex games is required. Paper materials (whether of posterboard, oak-tag board, index cards, etc.) can and should be laminated in advance of play to ensure their survival if repeated use is desired (clear contact paper or "seal" laminating film will suffice). Gameboards can be copied directly from the book. The easiest method is to use an opaque projector to project the board on a piece of posterboard taped to a wall. The gameboard can then simply be traced over the projected image. The choice of eraseable (Vis-A-Vis®) pens was made to facilitate repeated use of materials; non-eraseable (Sharpie®) pens are suggested when materials are to be of a permanent nature. (Any pens of similar quality can be used, of course.)

Once the materials are assembled, establishing basic procedures within the classroom can help to eliminate potential problems. The teacher or media specialist should explain the game to the students thoroughly at the outset and make sure that all students understand the rules before proceeding. Methods of determining order of play or choosing team leaders are not always suggested, as middle school students can determine these using their own methods. Some teachers or media specialists may want to monitor this activity to see that impartial methods are used. As for direction of play around the circle, going to the left or right is optional, naturally, so long as it is done consistently and does not confuse students or interfere with play. At the end of play, the teacher or media specialist will want to examine materials to be sure that all parts are present and in good enough repair to use again before storing the materials.

Careful and reflective use of *Media/Classroom Skills: Games for the Middle School, Vol. 1* will not only reward the teacher with a program of activities that presents students with the opportunity to learn; it will reward the media specialist with more teachers and students involved in the use of the IMC.

J.E.W.
I.W.B.

ACKNOWLEDGMENTS

In the preparation of this volume we have had invaluable aid from a number of media specialists and teachers who provided us access to their libraries and collections.

Ms. Alberta Barnett, Media Specialist, Carmody Junior High School, Jefferson County, Colorado.

Ms. Libby Berry, Media Specialist, Centennial Junior High School, Boulder County, Colorado

Ms. Frances Dufraine, Media Specialist, Baseline Junior High School (1979-1980); Boulder High School (1980-), Boulder County, Colorado

Ms. Marian Ramsey, Media Specialist, Merrill Junior High School, Denver County, Colorado

Mrs. Alice F. Silverberg, Art Teacher, Kepner Junior High School, Denver County, Colorado

Furthermore, we wish to express our appreciation to the following people for their ideas and encouragement:

Mr. Robert B. Brown
Ms. Kimberly Wieckert
Mr. Warren G. Wieckert

TABLE OF CONTENTS

NEW APPROACHES IN MEDIA INSTRUCTION

INFORMATION BANK: THE MEDIA CENTER

---

*Asterisks indicate those games that require little or no preparation time.

EXPRESSING THE MIND: LANGUAGE ARTS

MAN AND HIS ENVIRONMENT: SOCIAL STUDIES

WORLD COMMUNICATION: FOREIGN LANGUAGES

CREATIVE IMPRESSIONS: ART

NEW APPROACHES IN MEDIA INSTRUCTION

```
******************************************************************
```
THE NEED FOR A DIFFERENT APPROACH
```
******************************************************************
```

> We don't need no education
> We don't need no thought control
> No dark sarcasm in the classroom
> Teacher, leave those kids alone.
>
> —Pink Floyd, *The Wall*
> (Pink Floyd Music, Ltd., 1979)

The quiet rage of these words from a popular song reflect the feelings of boredom, hypocrisy, and hopelessness that many educators and students observe and experience in today's educational setting. This frustration and the feelings of futility have been well documented by Kozal,[1] Holt,[2] and Silberman.[3] What is the basis for these negative emotions? Students blame teachers, parents, and administrators. Parents blame students, peer pressure, teachers, and administrators. Administrators blame students, parents, and teachers. Teachers blame students, parents, administrators, drugs, apathy, or whatever, groping for some logical explanation of the difficult situations.

Today's generation is reacting to this frustration, the negativism, by simply leaving school. The middle schools, however, are in the unique position of having great numbers of students who are required by law to attend but who would prefer to be elsewhere, removed from the alleged destructive social conditioning of the schools. Since dropping out is not possible, acting out becomes the rule rather than the exception.

Solutions are sought by educators and parents, as alternative approaches to education are implemented. Precision teaching, programmed learning, affective education, learning centers, and humanistic education are a few of the techniques permeating the educational scene. The goals of these alternative forms of education are less restrictive and more humane classrooms that foster student involvement. Most of these alternatives share some basic ideas such as:[4]

- Students should have the right to pursue individual interests and activities.
- A need exists for students to be actively engaged with the enrivonment and with other people in order for meaningful learning to occur.
- Students learn at their own pace and with their own particular learning styles.
- Learning should be exciting and enjoyable.
- The instructor's role should be that of a diagnostician, guide, and inspirer.

Traditional methods are not effective for implementing the goals and objectives of today's educators and students. No longer can teachers only lecture to middle school students, expecting note taking, serious study, and completed homework assignments. Threats of poor grades, expulsion, and worse only serve to perpetuate and expand the problems.

HOW TO BRING ABOUT CHANGE

How then, can some of these problems and feelings be altered? A change in attitude and a plan for action enables one to release negative emotions. Changes do not come swiftly, or easily; however, a simple beginning can cause enough success to warrant additional changes.

The media specialist has an unparalleled opportunity to interact with faculty, students, parents, and administration to create a new educational perspective. The media center does not operate in isolation; it is an integral part of the total educational program and reflects the philosophy of the school and district administration. Prostano says that one of the primary elements of the media center program is planning and implementing curriculum:

> This thrusts the media professional into the educational scheme when new learning requirements are being developed and sustains the relationship through the practical day-to-day instructional program.[5]

Thus the media specialist can act as a catalyst to promote change.

An integrated approach to education with media specialists and teachers working in a cooperative effort to plan instructional programs is suggested for optimal results. Hopefully the media specialist can approach a teacher with the idea of using games to aid the teacher in getting students to assimilate information. If the information is given to the media specialist, a game can be produced and made available for use in the media center or for checkout. It would be wise of the media specialist to take the completed game to the teacher for a critique or for students to critique. As teachers find students more eager to utilize games for learning, perhaps teachers will be willing to provide ideas for games, to have students produce games, or even to produce games themselves.

This approach does take time and effort on the part of the media specialist and the teachers. Results, however, will help ease the frustration levels of teachers and students and draw more faculty and students into the media center. Results will warrant the investment of time. Time-saving ideas include using gifted and talented students to create formats, research information, and critique the game. Production of games can be arranged with art or shop teachers, having students prepare gameboards as class assignments. Parents and senior citizens might be involved as volunteers for production of games at home or at school.

The use of games is not suggested as the only technique for learning; it is one of many types of learning activities. The high level of motivation provided by the use of games actively involves students and provides a change of pace. Games can become as tedious as worksheets if used in isolation, without planning, and without evaluation procedures. Certainly, educators should introduce material, use additional learning activities, and evaluate the process and procedures utilized, using games as appropriate, supplemental learning activities.

Four major benefits of this method are:

- The student is allowed to function as an individual, in small groups and/or as a part of a team and has a wide range of alternative learning experiences.
- The method is designed for a media center approach to learning through individualization and independent learning, helps to promote these teaching/learning styles throughout the school.
- The media specialist is able to draw faculty and students from all subject areas into the media center.
- The media specialist can aid middle school teachers to move toward small group work and individualization.

Games are not the panacea for all the ills of education today. Games, however, can provide an approach to learning that can alter classroom climate for students yet provide an enjoyable technique for teachers.

GETTING INTO THE GAMING TECHNIQUE

The field of gaming is growing at a prodigious rate, as measured by the commercial availability of games and the creativity on the part of some educators. Yet reports indicate that games are not entering the classroom or media centers nearly as rapidly as one might suppose. Why is this? One can only speculate: "The term *game* connotes fun. And activities that are fun seem to be incompatible with activities that are serious."[6] Everyone knows that education is a serious business, and, therefore, games should not be used. Educational games, however, use the student's way of viewing things. They present concrete problems in a simplified but dramatic form that mediates between abstraction and confusion, between theory and reality. Yet they may be viewed as slightly upsetting phenomena by teachers who have never used them, seen them used, or learned from them. Even in this complex society many teachers have never been exposed to gaming in the course of their own education and training.

Gaming also depends upon a high degree of student cooperation, and some educators may have visions of wallowing in a turmoil of instructions, playing forms, role descriptions, charts, and discussion questions while their students "bounce off the walls in happy, screaming chaos, pretending to play a game."[7] This problem can be alleviated by proper selection of materials; students, at every ability level, can become deeply involved in the task assigned.

Games are also difficult to preview or review without playing them yourself. When you construct your own games, however, you (as an educator) are taking an active role in eliminating many of the fears or obstructions mentioned previously. For all of these reasons some concrete steps that educators could follow in constructing their own games are described below.

CONSTRUCTION OF GAMES

Step I – Develop the Theme. The place to start is where the need is the greatest. Access the curriculum to determine that need, keeping in mind the relationship between the game and real situations. As you work on selecting a theme ask yourself questions like these:

- Does the subject or theme relate to the school's or the media center's educational program?
- Is the educational value significant enough to warrant game construction?

Step II – Determine the Purpose. Write down some statements that clearly define the purpose and scope of the game. For example:

Purpose: To acquaint students with Sectionalism – its background, personalities, and conflict.

Scope: Our major interest is to examine whether a student would use an encyclopedia, a historical atlas or a historical dictionary to locate specific information.

Then decide whether the purpose of the game is to review or reinforce, to motivate or challenge, or to advance concept building or decision making.

Step III — Determine the Grade Level. Tailor the game so that the skills and information to be learned are geared to the range of abilities in the classroom. This ensures a better comprehension of the total process.

Step IV — Determine the Number of Players. Take into consideration how many students meet at any one time. Is it necessary to construct the game for a full class, one-half of the class, small groups, or a combination of the above. This step will affect the format, the type of materials to be used, and the procedure.

Step V — Determine the Format. The blueprint of the game will depend upon the goals and the needs and abilities of the students. At this time consider the competition involved; will it be competitive or non-competitive. The following are common formats:

- Board games — a graphic representation of the process under study and provision for players to keep track of their resources and their opponents.
- Card games — a game of chance by which two or more players interact to determine the outcome.
- Role playing — a teaching process involving bargaining, negotiating, or other human interactions.

Step VI — Determine the Method of Checking. Will the outcome of the game be checked by the media specialist, the librarian, the teacher, an aide or the student? If these methods are deemed too time consuming, an answer sheet or a method of self-checking (e.g., answers are on the back of cards which a team leader controls) are alternatives.

Step VII — Design and Gather the Materials. The design should bear a definite relationship to the established theme and/or purpose. It should be attractive, functional, and made from durable materials. At this point, you may want to introduce an element of chance such as: dice, spinners, playing cards, coins, and so on. Take into consideration what materials you will need for actual game construction: colored posterboard or paper; white posterboard or paper; flannel board and felt; books or magazines; a variety of manila envelopes; Vis-A-Vis®, Sharpie® or similar marking pens; scissors, glue, rubber bands, crayons; clear contact paper or laminating film; and so on. The possibilities are endless.

Step VIII — Define the Players' Roles. With the number of players already determined, describe their roles and the resources available to them. Perry Gillespie has written a functional description of different types of roles:[8]

- Individual roles — a person commands his or her own behavior and reaps the rewards or consequences of that behavior.
- Maintenance roles — a player acts as a messenger, a reference source, or an administrator.
- Task roles — a player must perform a specific task to win (e.g., use an encyclopedia, dictionary, map, and so on).

Step IX — Decide upon the Procedure and Time. Be exact about how the game is to be played; make the rules brief but clear. Inform the players what to do, who will interact with whom, what transactions will take place, and what the playing time will be. Will one class period be used for one round or can several rounds be fitted into one 45-50 minute period? Should the game be played all at once, or can it be split into convenient time blocks to fit a regular class schedule? Gillespie has also outlined seven classes of written procedural rules:[9]

- Initiation and Termination—state when a game begins and ends.
- Deployment and Desposition—indicate who, where, how and when a player can move.
- Communication—indicate if any kind of communication is permitted, restricted, and so on.
- Arbitration—indicate how disputes will be handled.
- Intervention—indicate if, and how, chance is introduced.
- Enforcement—indicate how infractions are covered.
- Rules of Outcome—indicate what conditions have to be met to win.

Step X—Trial Run. Play the game through to see if problems arise. If they do, iron them out. It is best to try the game on a small group first. Check to see if the mechanics of what you had in mind actually work. During this period observe and write down the problems that may be encountered. Do not be discouraged if the game does not work perfectly the first time. It may take several trial runs and some modifications before all details are satisfactory.

David Zuckerman and Robert Horn suggest several things to watch for during tryout:[10]

- How much time was devoted to each playing period? Was that enough?
- Did the game instructions work well? Suggest changes.
- Did the players play the roles easily or with difficulty?
- Were there players who were inactive during the play?
- Did the players have fun? Were they emotionally involved in the play?
- Does this game meet your educational objectives?

Step XI—Evaluation. Do not neglect or delegate this function to anyone else. One method of evaluation is through a postgame discussion. The very nature of a game suggests the need for a discussion during which the various activities that occurred can be brought together to describe a total picture. An important opportunity would be wasted if you simply returned to conventional activities without discussing those activities.

Begin the discussion with concrete and unthreatening kinds of question, with the determination of winners, or with scoring. The winning individual or team should be asked what actions they took in the game and why they thought these helped them to win. Similarly, individuals or teams that did not win can be asked to describe what they did, how they decided to take the actions they chose, and why these were less successful than those of the winning team. Other points to keep in mind are, what was learned, what difficulties were experienced, and what goals were met by playing the game.

WHY PLAY GAMES?

When educational games are developed, teachers and media specialists can exploit student energy for the business of learning. Games increase motivation, help the socialization process, clarify perplexing concepts, and integrate classes of diverse ability levels. If the gaming technique is used appropriately, the experience can be a rewarding one for both the student and the teacher or media specialist.

Motivation. To motivate is to "stimulate to action" or to "provide with an incentive." Students usually wish to be active, to participate, to make things happen rather than be passive spectators to events taking place around them. Unfortunately, the student is all too often lectured to or assigned to read a textbook by a teacher, assembled for more listening, fire-drilled, tested, and graded. If this were the only method, school could become boring, learning only temporary, and the desire to explore lost.

In contrast, as Gordon has pointed out (*Games for Growth*, 1970), games require active participation. Players manipulate colorful tokens, debate, bargain, negotiate, and make decisions; they make things happen. They are the causes of events, rather than creatures of the school environment. Educational games can provide students with a scaled-down model of the world over which influence and control can be exerted; they can serve as integral parts of teaching so that students do not become passive robots.

Immediate Feedback. Not only do game participants cause events; they know immediately what they have done. Feedback is not only prompt, but also natural. Success or failure is immediately apparent to the player; good strategy works. Actions and decisions are judged or reinforced along the same lines on which they were made. The student is not asked to accept on blind faith that the teacher knows what is best for him or her, or to wait for a test to be graded or for a teacher to approve or correct a verbal response.

Interaction. Students are social beings who love to talk with peers and they contain more energy than can be expended by sitting in class. Almost all educational games call for interaction among players—permitting or requiring physical movement around a gameboard or classroom. The chance to expend energy and the ability to communicate is thus an integral part of the learning experience. In games, what would normally be viewed as distractions are redirected to educational ends.

Competition and Cooperation. Many critics of games decry the element of competition. To be sure, competiveness can be destructive. Can these critics, however, overlook the fact that any school situation is inherently competitive? Students compete for grades, attention, parts in plays, positions on teams, and so on. There are always "winners" and "losers" though the labels may not be verbalized. All games are competitive to some extent and so are most people. Educational games thus exploit this inclination to compete and channel it for educational purposes.

Cooperation is a strong element of the very games that are competitive. Players on one team cooperate among themselves to compete with other teams. In games designed for individual roles rather than for teams, alliances spring up. Games thus tap the human instinct to cooperate in contrast to most conventional classroom activities, which demand individual performance and frequently penalize cooperation.

Position and Self-Image. In most classes a few leaders emerge and the other students expect them to give the correct answers, write the best papers, and receive the best grades. These "others" do not hope to achieve the same degree of success as the elite, and eventually they produce only a limited effort. In a game, there is no guarantee that the "good" student will win; there is no monopolization. Everyone participates at the same time. A combination of good decisions and good luck is required to win a game. The rewards do not depend on conformity to a teacher's rules of procedure, nor is there one right way of arriving at one right answer. Also, games are not graded in the way that other activities are, and this tends to remove inhibitions for some students. Finally, more leadership roles are offered than would normally be available in other classroom activities.

Gaining Information and Using Judgment. Information may appear in unorthodox forms, but facts are the basic material from which a game is built. Educators often have to coax, pressure, and implore students to make judgments about print and nonprint materials. Is the information accurate? Is it biased? Is it logical? Can it be used effectively? In playing a game, however, students implicitly evaluate their own actions and those of other players continuously. Success comes in the guise of good tactics or strategy. A player quickly discovers whether the tactics being used are effective. If they are not, reevaluation often takes place and ways are found to improve upon the strategy; thus the student gains a wealth of new information.

Problem Solving. Games are particularly well-suited for developing the problem-solving abilities of students. The purpose of the game may be to teach the expansion of vocabulary, recognition of sentence fragments, current events, countries of the world and their capitals, information found in the card catalog, use of the vertical file, and so on. Whatever the issue may be, it can be presented in the form of a problem that the player must contribute to solving. Many abilities are called into use in the game—the student must use his or her problem-solving faculties. Once a solution has been achieved (or the game completed), the steps used in reaching it can be reviewed and analyzed.

REWARDS

Research has shown that students are not motivated to improve poor grades, but are motivated to retain good grades. Grades can be equated with rewards or prizes, even though many educators are loathe to do so.

Rewards for winners of educational games can be as creative as the games themselves. Often, students will suggest rewards they would value highly, such as,

- a pass to the media center for "free" time
- being excused from a homework assignment
- being able to do a special job in the room
- being able to sit next to a friend in class for a week
- being able to chew gum in class

Other suggestions are:

- congratulatory notes—for example: Congratulations! You're a champ! You're the #1 team!
- coupons from fast-food restaurants for a free soft drink (some establishments will donate coupons)
- coupons for a discount admission to a local roller-rink or ice skating rink
- points toward a class trip or party

COORDINATION OF TEACHERS AND MEDIA SPECIALISTS

If the gaming technique is to be successful, both the teachers and the media specialist should plan together for classes, groups, and individuals to use the media center as their laboratory. It is unreasonable to expect that any one teacher or media specialist can single-handedly impart a large body of information to every student. An integration of media skills into subject area instruction is essential for it provides an immediate practical application for information that is often, in the students' opinion, esoteric. Together the teachers and the media specialist can give students guidance in exploring the resources, making selections, developing creative projects, and playing constructive games which require specific knowledge and skill. An attempt can be made to tailor the program to the needs of all, thereby giving everyone the opportunity to explore.

PRE-TEST AND POST-TEST

Cooperation between the media center and subject area departments can begin with pre-testing and post-testing. Students come into a middle school having had different levels of experience with the media center. One method of discovering on what level students are performing is to test them. This can be done most effectively through a subject area, especially language arts. Once it has been ascertained how well a student can function in a media center, a program can be worked out so that he or she learns to associate the media center with all subject areas. The following are a few suggestions of pre- and post-tests:

Pre- and Post-Test—1

Part I
To the left of the question number write the letter of the correct answer.

_____ 1. Books that are based on facts (factual) are called

    a. fiction   b. non-fiction   c. story collections

_____ 2. Books that are imaginary in nature are called

    a. reference books   b. non-fiction   c. fiction

_____ 3. The main use of the card catalog is to

    a. tell us how many pages the book has
    b. tell us who the author is
    c. tell us where to find the book

_____ 4. Mr. Dewey invented the Dewey Decimal System of Classification

    a. so we can tell the fiction from the non-fiction books
    b. so that books can be located and returned to the shelves more readily
    c. so that books of a like subject are together

_____ 5. A book in the 700s could be about

    a. football   b. flying an airplane   c. poetry

_____ 6. You can tell the subject card from the title card because

    a. the subject is always in capital letters
    b. the title is always in capital letters
    c. the subject card says "subject card" on it

_____ 7. Books in the non-fiction section of the library are put in order by

    a. the first two letters of the author's last name
    b. the number given to that particular book
    c. height

Part II
Select one tray from the card catalog and answer the following questions.

8. What are the outside guide letters on your tray? _____

9. What are the inside guides in your tray called? _____

10. Select one card from the catalog and fill in the following information:

  a. author _____
  b. title _____
  c. call number _____
  d. Is this book fiction or non-fiction? _____

11. Select four subject cards from the tray and write down those subjects:

  _____   _____
  _____   _____

12. Find cards for two books written by the same author.

  a. Name of the author _____
  b. Names of two books written by this author _____
                                                 _____

13. Select two non-fiction books from the tray and fill in the following:

  Call Number   Author   Title
  _____
  _____

14. Find an example of a cross-reference card. Copy that card on the lines below:

  _____
  _____

15. Below is a subject card which indicates on what pages material can be found. Using the sample, answer the following questions:

```
┌─────────────────────────────────────────────────────┐
│                                                      │
│           ATOMIC MEDICINE p. 150-58                  │
│                                                      │
│     500     Poole, Lynn                              │
│     P            Frontiers of Science.               │
│             McGraw-Hill, 1958.                       │
│                                                      │
│                                                      │
│                                                      │
│                                                      │
└─────────────────────────────────────────────────────┘
```

  a. List the subject _____
  b. What is the title of the book? _____
  c. What is the call number? _____
  d. On what pages would you find information on the subject? _____

Part III

Put an "F" on the line if the call number is fiction, and an "N" if it is non-fiction.

16. _____ 359   22. _____ Ref.
                Fer   973
                                           Tun

17. _____ 921   23. _____ Fic
                Cro   Mil

18. _____ Fic   24. _____ 636
                Lin   Tru

19. _____ Bio   25. _____ 921
                Denver,   Was
                John

20. _____ Fic   26. _____ 808.8
                Ort   Pin

21. _____ 998   27. _____ SC
                Tun

Pre- and Post-Test — 2

Part I

Indicate whether the following statements are true or false by writing "T" or "F" in the blanks.

_____ 1. Cards in the catalog are arranged alphabetically by the top line.

_____ 2. There is only one card in the catalog for each library book.

_____ 3. The title of a book is the first line of the author card.

_____ 4. The book, *The Story of Dr. Dolittle*, is filed under *T-h-e*.

_____ 5. If you know the title of a book, you can find out the author's name by finding the title card in the catalog.

_____ 6. To find how many books we have by a certain author, look up the author's last name in the catalog.

_____ 7. Books by Will James will be in the drawer that holds cards I-K.

_____ 8. There are guide letters both outside and inside the drawers showing which cards are in the drawer.

_____ 9. If you wish a book about Thomas A. Edison, look in the catalog drawer that contains the letter T.

_____ 10. If you are interested in reading on a certain subject, look up that subject in the catalog and you will find out what books on that subject are in the library.

_____ 11. There are many library books without cards in the catalog.

_____ 12. Author's names are filed last name first.

_____ 13. The Dewey Decimal System is used for fiction books.

_____ 14. The Dewey Decimal System divides all information books into 10 number classes (large).

_____ 15. Several books in the library may have the same classification number if they are about the same subject.

_____ 16. Non-fiction books are arranged in order according to the Dewey Decimal number.

_____ 17. 949 comes after 949 on the shelves.
         Mel   Wat

_____ 18. 398 comes after 398.2 on the shelves.
         Dol   Anr

_____ 19. 821 comes before 888 on the shelves.
         Cer   Fra

_____ 20. The table of contents serves as a brief outline of the content of the book.

_____ 21. The chief purpose of the cover is to protect the book.

_____ 22. The glossary is used to locate the page on which a subject appears in the book.

_____ 23. The index appears in the front of the book.

_____ 24. The table of contents appears in the front of the book.

_____ 25. The index is arranged in alphabetical order.

Part II

Identify the information asked for by using each type of card on this page.

A

```
F        Franklin, George Cory, 1892–
             Monte; illus. by Loretta &
         Prentice Philips.
         Houghton Mifflin, 1948.

             109p  illus.
```

B

```
             Monte

F        Franklin, George Cory, 1892–
             Monte; illus. by Loretta &
         Prentice Philips.
         Houghton Mifflin, c1948.

             109p  illus.
```

C

```
             BEARS–FICTION

F        Franklin, George Cory, 1892–
             Monte; illus. by Loretta &
         Prentice Philips.
         Houghton Mifflin, c1948.

             109p  illus.
```

26. Circle the call number on all three cards.

27. Fill in the blank with the correct letter:
Subject Card _____   Author Card _____   Title Card _____

28. Underline the title on all three cards.

29. Go to the card catalog, indicate in which drawer you would find each card:
Author Card _____   Title Card _____   Subject Card _____

30. Write the subject heading as it appears on the subject card. _____

31. Write the author's name as it appears on the author card. _____

32. Who is the book illustrated by? _____

33. Write the publishing company and the copyright date.
_____ & _____

34. Circle the paging.

Part III – Abbreviations
What do the following abbreviations mean?

35. Rev. or R _____

36. Bio or 92 _____

37. Fic or F _____

38. SC _____

39. SCI. FIC. _____

40. Can you find audiovisual materials listed in the card catalog?
Yes or No _____

Pre- and Post-Test – 3

Part I
Place the correct word or words in the blanks.

1. The classification system for materials used in school libraries is the _____ classification system.

2. In a library classification system, all books on the same _____ are placed together on the shelf.

3. Catalog cards are filed in _____ order.

Part II

The following are parts of a non-fiction book that you should know and make use of to find materials easily. Place the letters from Column B on the correct blanks in Column A.

Column A

_____ 4. an explanation of the purpose of the book.

_____ 5. author's full name

_____ 6. explanation of words used in the book

_____ 7. year the book was published

_____ 8. page on which a particular item may be found

_____ 9. additional charts or tables

_____ 10. person to whom the book is inscribed

_____ 11. a listing of chapters or sections in a book

_____ 12. list of books used for further reading

_____ 13. main portion of the book

Column B

A. Body
B. Title page
C. Table of Contents
D. Index
E. Appendix
F. Preface
G. Bibliography
H. Glossary
I. Dedication
J. Copyright date

Part III

Using the catalog card, write the names of the items identified by the arrows on the blanks provided.

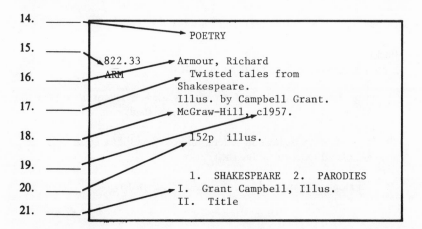

14. _____

15. _____

16. _____

17. _____

18. _____

19. _____

20. _____

21. _____

```
                        POETRY
  822.33      Armour, Richard
  ARM            Twisted tales from
             Shakespeare.
             Illus. by Campbell Grant.
             McGraw-Hill, c1957.

             152p  illus.


             1. SHAKESPEARE  2. PARODIES
             I.  Grant Campbell, Illus.
             II.  Title
```

22. You find that there are no books listed in the card catalog on the following subjects. What subject would you look under for each?
    a. drugs _____
    b. guns _____
    c. politics _____

Part IV

23. Mark the statement that best describes how you would search for periodical articles in a library or IMC.

    _____ Take off all of the periodicals from the shelves, sit on the floor, and begin going through them like crazy, hoping to find what you need for an assignment.

    _____ Go to the periodical index and look for the subject you need while the person who marked the above statement is sitting on the floor.

24. The periodical index for the most popular periodicals and the one you will probably use in junior high school or at the public library is called the _____.

    The following is a typical entry in this periodical index. Tell what each item is or means.

    Magnificent Apollo. E.K. Gann. *Flying.* 87:37-56 S '70

25. Magnificent Apollo is the _____.

26. E.K. Gann is the _____.

27. *Flying* is the _____.

28. 87 is _____.

29. 37-56 are _____.

30. S '70 is the _____.

31. The *Readers' Guide* and other periodical indexes perform much the same function for periodical articles (and you!) as the card catalog does for books. It is an _____ listing of the subjects, authors, and sometimes the titles of periodical articles.

Part V

In which of the reference books listed below would you look for the following?

_____ 32. The text of the Mayflower Compact.

_____ 33. A picture of a snowy owl.

_____ 34. Who said, "The walls have ears"?

_____ 35. The name of the book with the short story, *Mustang Kid.*

_____ 36. The name of the book with poem, "The Congo."

_____ 37. Where the author Madeline L'Engle lives.

_____ 38. The location of the city of Timbuktu.

_____ 39. What the animal called a Cony is.

_____ 40. How many books by Walter Farley are in this library?

_____ 41. How many died in the sinking of the Titanic?

A. World Almanac
B. Index to Poetry
C. Atlas
D. Something about the Authors
E. Index to Short Stories

F. Famous Quotations
G. Birds of America
H. Card Catalog
I. Parade of the Animal Kingdom
J. Documents of American History

CAREER GAME: PINNACLE POINT

Pinnacle Point is included here as an indication of the breadth and the usefulness of games in the middle school curriculum. It was designed for use in creating an awareness on the part of the students of the great number of careers related to each subject area taught in the middle school. The gameboard can be used in each subject area. A set of cards bearing information about careers related to a subject area will need to be substituted for each subject area. For example, art-related career information cards will be substituted when the art instructor requests the game, and foreign language-related career information cards will be substituted when the foreign language instructor requests the game. Lists of subject area related careers follow the game.

PINNACLE POINT

PURPOSE: To make students aware of the myriad careers available that are related to subject areas taught in a middle school.

GRADE LEVEL: 7th or 8th grade

TIME: 40 minutes

NUMBER: 4 students per gameboard

METHOD OF CHECKING: Self-checking

MATERIALS:
1) 1 Pinnacle Point gameboard for every four students playing.

2) 4 markers.

3) 1 die.

4) 30 3x4-inch colored posterboard cards bearing information about careers. The examples below refer to careers that are related to the language arts. The same type of cards can be made to apply to any curriculum area.

You must have four years of college to become an English teacher – pay $20,000.
A publisher must do promotional work – pay $1,500 for a convention trip.
A journalist must sometimes travel – collect $500 for a short trip.
Pay day for a television announcer – collect $2,000.

(Materials list continues on page 40)

As an author, you collect $4,000 in royalties on a book.

As a media specialist, you must take additional classes to maintain your certificate — pay $300.

5) Play money in $100, $500, and $1,000 denominations (100 of each).

6) Paper and pencil.

7) Large manila envelope (16x20-inches) for the materials.

PROCEDURE:

1) Players are given a Pinnacle Point gameboard and related materials.

2) Markers are placed on start, cards are shuffled and placed face down in a pile in the appropriate space on the gameboard, and the die is rolled to determine order or play. One player is chosen to be the banker.

3) Each player is given $2,000. The first player rolls the die and moves the number of spaces indicated by the die. If the player lands on a space marked with a stick of dynamite, a card is drawn and read aloud, directions are followed, and the card is placed in a discard pile. If a player lands on a space with directions, those directions must be followed.

4) If a player receives directions to pay an amount of money which he or she does not have, the bank may make a loan to be collected when the player reaches Pinnacle Point. The banker keeps a record of the loans on a piece of paper.

5) Play continues with players alternating turns. Any player rolling a six, moves six spaces and collects $1,000.

6) As players approach the top of Pinnacle Point, a correct number on the die must be rolled for a final move.

7) The players continue the game until all players reach Pinnacle Point.

8) The player with the most money wins.

* * *

Career Lists

Library Science Careers

The following is a suggested list of occupational opportunities for those trained in librarianship, some of which require more, and some less, than four years of study.

Media specialist	University librarian
Media technician	Book reviewer
Cataloger	Professor of library science
Medical librarian	Medical records librarian
Reference librarian	Young adult librarian
Government documents librarian	Company librarian
Bookbinder	Library clerk
Printer	Library technical assistant
Publisher	Legal librarian
Computer programmer	Storyteller
Children's librarian	Shelver of books
Library administrator	Rare books librarian

Language Arts Careers

The following list is distributed by the Career Education Resource Center (2323 W. Baker Ave., Englewood, CO 80110).

Academic research assistant	Actor/actress
Administrative assistant	Advertising copywriter
Advertising traffic manager	Archivist
Auctioneer	Audiologist
Bilingual teacher	Biographer
Book buyer	Book reviewer
Clipping service worker	College English teacher
College registrar	College teacher
Columnist	Continuity writer
Copy editor	Correspondence clerk
Court reporter	Critic
Dean of women/men	Director of admissions
Disc jockey	Drama teacher
Editor	Editorial assistant
File clerk	Foreign service officer
Foreign service secretary	Fund raiser
Ghostwriter	Home economist
Industrial journalist	Interpreter
Job analyst	Judge
Kindergarten/elementary teacher	Lawyer
Legal assistant	Lexicographer
Librarian	Library technical assistant
Literary agent	Literary writer
Mathematics coordinator	Medical record librarian
Medical secretary	Minister (protestant)
Motion picture producer	Narrator
Newscaster	News correspondent
News photographer	Newspaper editor
Newspaper reporter	Personnel manager
Playwright	Politician

(Language Arts Careers list continues on page 42)

Language Arts Careers (cont'd)

Postal service worker
Proofreader
Public relations worker
Publisher's sales representative
Radio and television announcer
Reading consultant
Receptionist
Rewrite person
Scenario writer
Science fiction writer
Secondary school teacher
Singer
Speech pathologist
Sportscaster
Stenographer
Teacher aide
Technical writer
Television director
Training representative
Typesetter
Writer, juvenile literature

Priest (Roman Catholic)
Public information officer
Publicity director, publishing
Rabbi
Reader
Reading specialist
Research account exec., advertising
Sales manager
School principal
Scientific linguist
Secretary
Special education teacher
Speechwriter
Sports writer
Superintendent of schools
Teacher of English/second language
  ESL
Telephone operator
Title examiner
Translator
Typist

Social Studies Careers

The following list was taken from *User's Guide for Social Studies: Career Opportunities* (Boston, MA: Houghton Mifflin, 1975).

Anthropologist
Archaelogist
Architectural restoration specialist
Cartographer
Caseworker
Child psychologist
City manager
Clinical psychologist
College career planning &
  placement counselor
Counseling psychologist
Criminologist
Dean of women/men
Developmental psychologist
Drug counselor
Economist
Educational psychologist
Employment counselor
Employment interviewer
Ethnologist
Geographer
Elementary and secondary school
  teacher
Historian
Historic sites supervisor
Industrial and labor relations
  director

Industrial psychologist
Industrial sociologist
Job analyst
Judge
Lawyer
Legal assistant
Literary writer
Museum curator
Market research analyst
Medical social worker
Penologist
Psychiatrist
Political scientist
Psychiatric social worker
Peace corps volunteer
Psychologist
Political geographer
Politician
Public relations worker
Probation officer
Relocation specialist
Rural sociologist
School counselor
School social worker
School psychologist
Sociologist
Social ecologist

Social pathologist
Social psychologist
Social studies editor

Social worker
Urban planner
Urban sociologist

Foreign Language Careers

This list of occupations related to foreign language study was compiled by the Career Education Resource Center (2323 W. Baker Ave., Englewood, CO 80110).

Airline ground receptionist
Airline steward/stewardess
Anthropologist
Archaeologist
Archivist
Art historian
Bilingual legal secretary
Bilingual medical secretary
Bilingual secretary
Bilingual ski instructor
Bilingual teacher
Biographer
Border patrol agent
Cartographer
Caseworker
College teacher of comparative
    literature
College teacher of foreign
    languages and literatures
Cookbook compiler
Customs inspector
Documentary film maker
Editor of standardized foreign
    language tests
Employment counselor
Ethnologist
Etymologist
Flight purser
Foreign buyer
Foreign clerk
Foreign corresondent
Foreign exchange clerk
Foreign language correspondence
    clerk
Foreign language editor
Foreign language proofreader
Foreign language stenographer
Foreign language teacher
Foreign service information officer
Foreign service officer
Foreign service secretary
Geographer
Historian
Home health aide

Hotel front office clerk
Hotel manager
Immigration inspector
Import-export agent
Intelligence specialist
International banking officer
International advertising copywriter
International broadcast announcer
International lawyer
International manufacturer's
    representative
International market research analyst
International public relations worker
International receptionist
International relations specialist
International social welfare agency
    worker
International trade economist
Interpreter
Lexicographer
Librarian
Management aide (housing)
Minister (protestant)
Missionary
Museum curator
Music librarian
Newspaper reporter
Peace Corps volunteer
Philologist
Police officer
Precis writer
Priest (Roman Catholic)
Public health nurse
Rabbi
Reader
Recreation director
Scientific linguist
Singer
Sociologist
Translator
Translator, scientific documents
Travel agent
Travel guide
Travel guidebook writer

(Foreign Language Careers list continues on page 44)

Foreign Language Careers (cont'd)

Travelers information service worker
Urban sociologist
Vista volunteer

Art Careers

The following is a suggested list of occupational opportunities for those trained in art, some of which require more, and some less, than four years of study.

Advertising layout person	Fashion artist
Advertising person	Fashion columnist
Art appraiser	Fashion coordinator
Art historian	Furniture designer
Art layout person	Furniture reproducer
Art teacher	Graphic artist
Ceramist	Illustrator
Cartoonist, motion pictures	Illustrator, advertising
Cartoonist, newspaper and magazine	Illustrator, book
Color coordinator	Illustrator, catalog
Color expert	Illustrator, children's books
Commercial artist	Illustrator, costume
Commercial decorator	Illustrator, magazine
Commercial designer	Illustrator, newspaper
Commercial letterer	Illustrator, production
Costume designer	Librarian, art
Curator, art gallery	Lithographer, artist
Decorator	Map maker
Designer	Model maker, industrial
Designer, book	Motion picture scenic artist
Designer, fashion	Motion picture art director
Designer, interior	Motion picture art researcher
Designer, jewelry	Mural painter
Designer, textile	Painter, miniature
Director, art	Painter, portrait
Director, costume	Painter, still-life
Director, fashion	Painter, water color
Display artist	Pattern designer
Draftsman	Photo-cartographer
Editor, art	Scientific artist
Editor, fashion	Sculptor
Embroidery designer	Silk-screen printer
Engraver, block	Silversmith
Engraver, copperplate	Sports cartoonist
Engraver, flatware	Stage designer
Engraver, jewelry	

FOOTNOTES

[1]Jonathan Kozal, *Death at an Early Age* (Boston: Houghton Mifflin, 1967).

[2]John Holt, *How Children Fail* (New York: Pitman, 1964).

[3]Charles E. Silberman, *Crisis in the Classroom* (New York: Random House, 1970).

[4]Barbara Blitz, *The Open Classroom: Making It Work* (Boston: Allyn and Bacon, 1973).

[5]Emanuel T. Prostano and Joyce S. Prostano, *The School Library Media Center* (Littleton, CO: Libraries Unlimited, 1977).

[6]Alice Kaplan Gordon, *Games for Growth* (Palo Alto, CA: Science Research Associates, 1970), p. 3.

[7]David Zuckerman and Robert Horn, *Guide to Simulation: Games for Education and Training* (Cranford, NJ: Didactic Systems, 1977), p. 502.

[8]Perry S. Gillespie, *A Model for the Development of Academic Games* (Ann Arbor, MI: University Microfilms, 1976), p. 78-85.

[9]Gillespie, *A Model*, p. 93-102.

[10]Zuckerman and Horn, *Guide to Simulation*, p. 512.

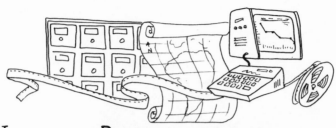

INFORMATION BANK: THE MEDIA CENTER

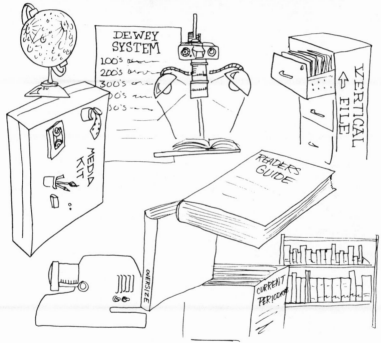

****
ROCKOLA
****

PURPOSE: To review alphabetizing of words.

GRADE LEVEL: 7th or 8th grade

TIME: 20 minutes

NUMBER: 1 player per Rockola card

METHOD OF CHECKING: Self-checking

MATERIALS:
1)   1 Rockola card for each student playing made from 11x14-inch tagboard.

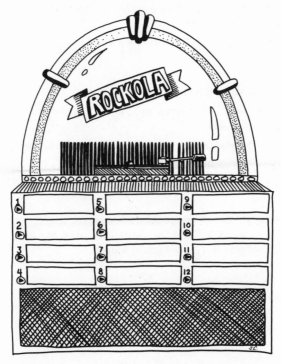

2)   3 sets of 12 (½x2½-inch) tagboard strips per card bearing names of popular musical performers, groups, and/or popular songs. For example:

Beatles	"Oldtime Rock and Roll"
"Lido Shuffle"	Bob Seger
Boz Scaggs	"Fire Lake"
"Fire on the Mountain"	Doobie Brothers
"Lady Madonna"	"Revolution"
"Yellow Submarine"	Grateful Dead
"Desperado"	"Like a Rolling Stone"
Eagles	"Stairway to Heaven"
"Life in the Fast Lane"	Led Zeppelin

(Materials list continues on page 50)

Ask students to suggest groups and titles prior to playing the game; this will result in a list that is popular with the class. An easy math problem should be written on the reverse side of the strips with the answer equal to the position of the strip on the card. For example, the strip printed below should occupy the second position on the card.

BEATLES

(Front)

$3 - 1 =$ ☐
Set A

(Back)

It is also helpful to label each set of strips (Set A, Set B, etc.) for ease in sorting. Each set should be banded together.

3) Large manila envelope (16x20-inches) for the materials.

PROCEDURE:

Form A

1) Two students are given Rockola cards and strips.

2) The students choose 1 set of strips and race to alphabetize the strips in the appropriate spaces on the card.

3) When finished, the students exchange cards and check the reverse side of the strips.

4) The first player to alphabetize the set correctly wins the first round.

5) The player who wins two out of three rounds, wins the game.

Form B

Played the same as Form A except the students in the class are arranged in pairs with consideration as to ability, and the entire class plays the game. Winners may be matched with winners to find the grand winner.

* * *

```
********************************************************************
```
ALPHABETIZING WITH THE AUTHORS
```
********************************************************************
```

PURPOSE: To develop students' ability to alphabetize actual books by the author's name and to shelve them with the collection on the shelves.

GRADE LEVEL: 7th or 8th grade

TIME: 15-20 minutes per round

NUMBER: Best played with a maximum of 16 students (even number required)

METHOD OF CHECKING: Media specialist

MATERIALS:
1) A stack of 14 books for every two students (total to be determined by the number of students playing at any one time).

2) 2 bookends for every pair of students.

3) 14 strips (posterboard, paint chips, paint sticks, and so on) for every two students, one to be placed in each book.

PROCEDURE:
1) One stack of 14 books is placed on a flat surface for every two students participating.

2) Working in pairs, students alphabetize these between the bookends according to author's last name.

3) When finished, students raise hands and the media specialist checks to see if the books are correctly alphabetized. If not correct, students continue work until they are correct.

4) If correct, the students involved attempt to shelve the books (alphabetically by author's last name) with the collection on the shelves. A strip juts out of each book thus shelved so the media specialist may check it.

5) For each stack correctly alphabetized the first time, students score two points; one point thereafter. For each book correctly shelved, each student receives one point.

6) More than one round may be played if time allows or more practice is needed.

* * *

IMC ABCs

PURPOSE: To broaden students' knowledge of the resources available in the media center.

GRADE LEVEL: 7th grade

TIME: 30 minutes

NUMBER: 2-16 students

METHOD OF CHECKING: Media specialist and/or teacher

MATERIALS:
1)   Pencils and paper for each team.

PROCEDURE:
1)   The group is divided into 2 teams and captains are chosen.

2)   The captains are given a piece of paper and a pencil and become the recorders for the teams.

3)   The individuals on the team work together for 15 minutes listing as many resources of the media center as possible, arranged under the letters of the alphabet. For example:

A — Art prints
    Adventure stories

B — Book talks
    Black History

C — Cassettes
    Consumer information

D — Dewey Decimals
    Detective stories

E — Encyclopedias
    Ear phones

Individuals may use the card catalog and other materials in the media center.

4)   After 15 minutes the teams come together in order to score the papers. The media specialist asks each team to read the list for each letter.

5)   For each resource listed, the team scores a point.

6)   The team with the highest score wins.

* * *

```
************************************************************
```
DO YOU KNOW YOUR BOOKS???
```
************************************************************
```

PURPOSE: To review the parts of a book and to develop speed in deciding their location.

GRADE LEVEL: 7th or 8th grade

TIME: 45 minutes

NUMBER: 6-8 players per gameboard

METHOD OF CHECKING: Self-checking

MATERIALS:
1) 1 gameboard made from 22x28-inch colored posterboard. Divide into 3 unequal sections and label, as shown below:

```
+-------------------------------------------+
|        DO YOU KNOW YOUR BOOKS ???         |
+-------------------------+-----------------+
|    BEGINNING - 1        |   MIDDLE -2     |
|                         |                 |
|                         |                 |
|                         |                 |
|                         +-----------------+
|                         |   END - 3       |
|                         |                 |
|                         |                 |
|                         |                 |
+-------------------------+-----------------+
```

2) 42 3x4-inch colored posterboard cards numbered on the backs from 1 to 42. On the front of each card, letter one of the parts of a book from the following list:

Beginning	Middle	End
title page	chapter headings	index of authors
author	chapter questions	footnotes
dedication	story illustrations	glossary
editor	chapter bibliography	index
prologue	narrative poems	epilogue
frontispiece	chapters	appendix
acknowledgements	poems	index of titles
edition	plays	author synopsis
index abbreviations	orations	index of first lines
title	articles	bibliography for the entire
list of illustrations	footnotes	book

(Materials list continues on page 54)

Beginning	**Middle**
illustrator	essays
place of printing	stories
translator	running titles
table of contents	
publishing company	
copyright date	
foreword	

3) 42 3x4-inch colored posterboard cards for the team leader to use. They should have the same numbers and terms on them as is printed on the other set. This time, however, the number is on the front and the answer is on the back with its proper number (corresponding to beginning-1; middle-2; end-3) in the lower right-hand corner.

4) Large manila envelope (12x15-inches) for the materials.

PROCEDURE:

1) Six to eight players gather around a table and choose a team leader.

2) The gameboard is placed on the table, player cards given to the players, and team cards given to the team leader.

3) The team leader picks one of the team cards and holds it up with the number facing the players (the answer toward the leader).

4) The player holding that number takes his or her player card and places the card on the appropriate section of the gameboard (1, 2, or 3), term side facing up.

5) If correct, it stays there. If incorrect, the team leader takes the card and uses it for review at the end of the game.

6) Play continues with the leader displaying team cards to be matched by player cards until all cards are used.

7) For each card placed correctly, a player scores one point.

* * *

```
********************************************************************
```
C. C. SEARCH
```
********************************************************************
```

PURPOSE: To allow students to demonstrate the ability to recognize subjects and to locate information in the card catalog on those subjects.

GRADE LEVEL: 7th or 8th grade

TIME: 2 class periods of 50 minutes each

NUMBER: Small group to an entire class

METHOD OF CHECKING: Media specialist

MATERIALS:
1) Newspaper clippings (articles and pictures) representing as varied a field of subjects as possible.

2) Colored paper of all sizes and shapes. Dry-mount the newspaper items to the colored paper, then laminate; these are "C. C. Search" cards.

3) Paper, call stips, and pencils for each student.

4) Large manila envelope (16x20-inches) for the materials.

PROCEDURE:
1) Divide the students into evenly matched teams, and choose a leader for each.

2) Place an equal number of "C. C. Search" cards on each table around which team members are gathered.

3) Members of the teams discuss under what subject they are to look in the card catalog for the topic of each "C. C. Search" card.

4) Once the subjects have been determined and a list made, team members should pass the list around the table making their own list of at least 10 items. When the lists are complete, players go to the card catalog.

5) Players locate the necessary information in the card catalog; write on call slips the author, title, and call number of an item on that topic; locate the item; and bring it back to the media specialist.

6) When the items have been checked by the media specialist, they are returned to the correct positions on the shelves.

* * *

```
********************************************************************
```
C. C. BINGO
```
********************************************************************
```

PURPOSE: To review the information found on an author card, title card, or subject card.

GRADE LEVEL: 7th or 8th grade

TIME: 15-20 minutes per round

NUMBER: Small group to an entire class

METHOD OF CHECKING: Media specialist and students

MATERIALS:

1) 1 large call sheet that has one category of information to be found on a catalog card under each letter. Size will depend upon how much information will be reviewed.

2) 1x2-inch colored posterboard call tokens to be placed on the master sheet after a term has been mentioned.
   For example:

   B—Publisher   N—Author's name
   I—Copyright date   G—Call number
                                                  O—Title

3) Enough 5x6-inch colored posterboard "C. C. Bingo" cards for each student playing. Each card should be different and have the categories written at random. Highlight the words AUTHOR CARD, TITLE CARD, and SUBJECT CARD when used.

"C. C."

B I N G O

PUBLISHER	TRANSLATOR	PLACE OF PUBLICATION	SUBJECT	AUTHOR'S NAME
ILLUSTRATION	COPYRIGHT DATE	ILLUSTRATOR'S NAME	*Author Card*	NUMBER OF PAGES
SUMMARY	PSEUD.	FREE	PUBLISHER	TITLE
AUTHOR'S NAME	*Title Card*	NUMBER OF PAGES	ILLUSTRATOR'S NAME	SUMMARY
TITLE	ILLUSTRATIONS	PLACE OF PUBLICATION	COPYRIGHT DATE	*Subject Card*

4) 25 plastic tokens, buttons, and so on for each player.

5) Several transparencies of typical card catalog cards with overlays.

6) Overhead projector and screen.

7) 1 pointer.

(Materials list continues on page 58)

8) Large manila envelope (16x20-inches) for the materials.

PROCEDURE:

1) Each student is given one "C. C. Bingo" card and 25 plastic tokens or buttons.

2) Set up the overhead projector and put the transparency to be used in place.

3) The media specialist places the call tokens in a box or bowl to use in drawing terms to point out.

4) The media specialist draws one call token, reads the letter, and points to a category on the transparency. For example: "I — 1980."

5) Each player looks at the appropriate row on his or her "C. C. Bingo" card (in this case, the row below "I"). If the correct category (in the example, copyright date) appears in that row on the player's card, the player covers it with a plastic token or button.

6) The media specialist places the call token in the corresponding space on the call sheet, draws another, and goes through the same procedure.

7) Inform the students ahead of time that when the AUTHOR, TITLE, or SUBJECT CARD is asked for, the entire card will be outlined on the transparency with the pointer.

8) Play continues in this manner until a player covers 5 correct categories in a row — vertically, horizontally, or diagonally — and calls "Bingo."

9) Once "Bingo" has been called, no other player may place a token or button on his or her card until the original has been checked for accuracy.

10) For accuracy's sake, the winner should read off the categories covered so that the media specialist can check them against the categories covered on the call sheet.

11) The winning player in each instance is to receive a certain number of points — to be determined by the media specialist.

12) Variations of the game include:
    a) Four Corners — All four corners must be covered with tokens or buttons to win.
    b) Picture Frame — All squares on the outside of the card must be covered with tokens or buttons to win.
    c) Black-Out — All squares must be covered with tokens or buttons to win.

13) For a more difficult version of the game, use the type of "C. C. Bingo" card found on page 59.
    a) Steps one and two are the same as above. The transparencies and overhead will be used only for the AUTHOR, TITLE, or SUBJECT CARDS.
    b) The media specialist places the call tokens in a box or bowl to use in drawing terms to call out.
    c) The media specialist draws one call token, reads the letter and category printed on it (for example, "G — author's name").
    d) Each player looks at the appropriate row on his or her "C. C. Bingo" card (in this case, the row below "G"). If the name/term that is called (in the example, Bell, Irene) appears in that row on the player's card, the player covers it with a plastic token or button.

e) Steps 6 through 12 are the same.

"C.C."

B	I	N	G	O
Author Card	Bell, Irene	The Outsiders	il. by Jay Conley	Houghton Mifflin
Erick Berry [pseud.]	Boston:	c 1980	BASEBALL-BIOGRAPHY	Subject Card
UNP	940.5 Duprey	FREE	Wieckert, Jeanne	Describes the Negro's role as ...
WITCHCRAFT FICTION	Scribner's	Title Card	c 1979	New York:
BIO FLACK, ROBERTA	il. by Earl Goodenow	258 p.	The Old West Speaks	Story of Thistle B, a Canary

* * *

****

DEWEY AT THE BAT

****

PURPOSE: To review the various types of information that fall within the scope of the Dewey Decimal Classification System.

GRADE LEVEL: 7th or 8th grade

TIME: 15-20 minutes per inning

NUMBER: 9 players per team

METHOD OF CHECKING: Answer sheet

MATERIALS:

1) 1 set of bases and a homerun plate — total of 4 cloth bags or posterboard cards. A chalkboard with a baseball diamond may also be used.

2) 1 timer or stop watch.

3) Several master lists of questions, statements or directions with answers when applicable; dry-mounted to a piece of colored posterboard. For example:

Single (answer in 20 seconds)
a) Name the three types of cards found in the card catalog for each book.
b) Choose a non-fiction book from the collection, turn to the title page and read 5 important pieces of information found on that page.
c) Using the same book, name the publishing company and the copyright date.
d) Again using the same book, find the table of contents and index if the book contains the same.

Double (answer in 30 seconds)
a) Go to the card catalog and find the title of any biography on baseball and write down its title.
b) Look in any dictionary and find a definition of democracy, bring it back and read it to the teams.
c) From an author card for S. E. Hinton in the card catalog, find out how many pages *That Was Then, This Is Now* has.
d) Using any reference book available, find a map of China; bring it back for the teams to see.

Triple (answer in 40 seconds)
a) Look in *Collier's Encyclopedia* and find the author of the article on "Musical Instruments"; write it down.
b) Find the main entry card for *Dragons in the Waters*; who is the author?
c) Using the *Rand McNally Cosmopolitan World Atlas*, find the population of the capital city of Czechoslovakia; write it down.
d) Locate a non-fiction book on SUPERSTITION and retrieve it from the shelf.

Home Run (answer in 60 seconds)
a) Look in the *World Almanac* and find the presidential election returns for the state of Massachusetts in 1976; tell how many people voted for Jimmy Carter and how many voted for Gerald Ford.
b) Using the *Guinness Book of World Records*, find the name and age of the youngest author; share the information with the teams.

    c) Does the media center have any information on the Sioux Indians? If so, give the author and title of one fiction book and one non-fiction book.

    d) Go to the card catalog and look up the call number for a book on RUNNING by Don Conham. Go to the shelf and if the book is there, bring it back and show it to the teams.

4)   Large manila envelope (16x20-inches) for the materials.

PROCEDURE:

1)   Divide the students into two evenly matched teams and choose a captain for each team.

2)   Appoint two umpires and one timekeeper who will also keep score.

3)   Decide on the locations for first, second, and third bases and home plate. Place them in position.

4)   Team members line up behind their captains.

5)   The media specialist will be the pitcher and will "pitch" the questions, statements, or directions.

6)   In this version, there are no strikes—only outs, hits, and runs.

7)   A hit and consequently a run are made by the player answering a question, statement or following a direction correctly. The single, double, triple, or home run depends on the choice of questions, statements or directions. The difficulty varies, a single is the easiest while a home run is the most difficult.

8)   If the student fails to answer the question, statement or perform the direction in the given time limit, it is an out and he or she goes to the end of the line-up.

9)   Each correct answer advances the player or players until home plate is reached when a run is scored.

10)   When a player has rounded all bases, he or she goes to the end of the lineup until his or her turn "at bat" comes up again.

11)   Team one continues until it gets three outs (three wrong answers): then team two has a turn at bat.

12)   Teams alternate play in this manner.

13)   There are three outs for each team in an inning and as many innings can be played as time permits or as long as the interest level is maintained.

14)   The team that has scored the most runs at the end of the game is the winner.

* * *

```
***********************************************************
```
SHUFFLE ALONG WITH DEWEY
```
***********************************************************
```

PURPOSE: 1) To display a knowledge of the Dewey Decimal Classification System and independently to locate books; 2) to help students realize that each subject group contains much varied information.

GRADE LEVEL: 7th or 8th grade

TIME: 2 class periods of 50 minutes each

NUMBER: Small group to an entire class

METHOD OF CHECKING: Media specialist

MATERIALS:
1) Newspaper clippings (articles and pictures) representing as great a variety of subjects as possible; dry-mounted on colored paper; these are "Dewey Shuffle" cards.

2) Dewey Decimal Classification System bookmarks or dittoed sheets.

3) Colored strips (colored posterboard, paint chips, or paint sticks) for each student, one to be placed in each book.

4) Large manila envelope (16x20-inches) for the materials.

PROCEDURE:
1) Divide the students into evenly matched teams and choose a leader for each.

2) Place an equal number of "Dewey Shuffle" cards on each table around which team members are gathered.

3) The cards are to be sorted by the teams into stacks representing the different subject or classification groups (500s, 600s, 700s, and so on).

4) Team members check the stacks of cards carefully to determine that all is correct (with the help of the bookmarks or dittoed sheets).

5) The team leader raises a hand when all is finished.

6) The media specialist checks the card stacks and determines the number of points that a team has scored.

7) Each team member records at least eight items from its stack along with the broad classification number.

8) Discuss all of the different categories found within each subject group.

9) When the discussion is finished, players go to the card catalog; locate the subjects; write on a call slip the author, title, and call number of an item on that topic; locate the item on the shelves; and bring it back to the media specialist.

10) When the items have been checked by the media specialist, they are returned to the correct positions on the shelves. A colored strip is placed in each item before it is reshelved so the media specialist may check it.

11) For each book correctly shelved, each student receives one point.

* * *

```
*************************************************************
```
DICTIONARY BLUFF
```
*************************************************************
```

PURPOSE: To promote familiarity with unusual words and definitions.

GRADE LEVEL: 7th grade

TIME: 20 minutes

NUMBER: 4 to 6 students

METHOD OF CHECKING: Self-checking with any disputes settled by the media specialist or teacher

MATERIALS:
1) 1 dictionary.
2) Paper and pencil for score keeping.

PROCEDURE:
1) Players determine who is to take the first turn.
2) Player number one skims through the dictionary to find an unusual word and reads the word aloud. (If necessary the word may also be spelled.)
3) Each of the other players gives a definition for the word when called upon by player number one.
4) If the definition is unknown by a player, a nonsense definition may be invented.
5) Player number one reads the correct definition.
6) Each player who gives the correct definition receives 10 points.
7) The next turn goes to the first player to give correct definition.
8) If no correct definitions are given, player number one gives the correct definition, receives 5 points, and chooses another word.
9) The winner is the player with the most points after 20 minutes of play.

* * *

SYNONYM SEARCH

PURPOSE: To develop mastery and speed in using a dictionary to locate synonyms.

GRADE LEVEL: 7th or 8th grade

TIME: 30 minutes

NUMBER: 2 players per gameboard

METHOD OF CHECKING: Self-checking with disagreements settled by the media specialist or teacher

MATERIALS:
1) A Synonym Search gameboard for every two students; 8½x11½-inch oak-tag.

SYNONYM SEARCH		

2) 10 3x4-inch colored posterboard cards each bearing a word. For example:

accumulate	auxiliary
barbarous	commemorate
demonstration	endeavor
illiterate	supersede
valiant	villain

3) 2 Vis-A-Vis® pens of different colors.

4) 1 dictionary for each player.

5) Damp paper towels.

6) Large manila envelope (12x15-inches) for the materials.

PROCEDURE:
1) Each pair of students is given a Synonym Search gameboard, the Vis-A-Vis® pens, cards, and dictionaries. (Players should be closely matched in ability to use a dictionary.)

2) The first player shuffles the cards, places them at the top of the gameboard, and turns the top card face up. Both players race to find the word in the dictionary.

3) The player who is first to find the word writes a synonym for that word in any space on the gameboard. The other player may challenge by asking to see the synonym in the dictionary. If the disagreement persists, the teacher or media specialist can be asked to make a decision.

4) The word card is placed at the bottom of the pile and the second player turns another card face up.

5) Play continues in this manner until one player fills three spaces; vertically, horizontally or diagonally.

6) The gameboard is wiped clean and players begin again. The player who wins 2 out of 3 games is the winner.

7) The players may be matched by ability, and winners may be matched with winners to find the "Grand Winner."

* * *

WHO DONE IT???

PURPOSE: To develop a familiarity with the guide words of an encyclopedia.

GRADE LEVEL: 7th or 8th grade

TIME: 45 minutes

NUMBER: Small group to an entire class

METHOD OF CHECKING: Answer sheet

MATERIALS:

1) 50 4x4-inch colored posterboard "clue" cards.

```
ENCYCLOPEDIA AMERICANA...1980

    Burma to Cathay (5)


Who
Where
Weapon

656,    237,    625
```

On the back of each card, in the lower right-hand corner, place a number (1-50); number to correspond to those used on answer sheet.

2) Set of encyclopedias — clues for this game are based upon *Encyclopedia Americana*, c1980.

3) Pencils and paper.

4) Master list of clues; dry-mounted to pieces of colored posterboard. List the clues according to the number on the cards (see materials 1). For example:

656 — Caribbean 625 — carbon dioxide 237 — Calvin, John

5) Large manila envelope (12x15-inches) for the materials.

PROCEDURE:

1) Place the clue cards face down on a table.

2) Each player chooses a card and retrieves the volume of the encyclopedia mentioned on the card.

3) The object of the game is to discover the answers to these three questions:

   a) Who did it?
   b) Where did the event take place?
   c) What weapon was used?

4) The answers are to be found in the guide words located at the top of the encyclopedia pages marked on the clue cards.

5) The guide words will tell who did it, and reveal the place where it happened and the weapon used.

6) Form the clues into an imaginative sentence. For example: John Calvin was in the Caribbean giving a series of sermons when he was overcome by carbon dioxide.

7) When five clue cards have been completed, the player may help someone who is having trouble.

8) For each clue correctly identified, the player scores one point. Depending upon the quality of the sentence, from one to three points may be given.

* * *

SEEK OUT AND FIND

PURPOSE: To allow students to demonstrate the ability to use an encyclopedia by successfully locating specific information.

GRADE LEVEL: 7th or 8th grade

TIME: 45-50 minutes

NUMBER: Small group to an entire class

METHOD OF CHECKING: Media specialist and/or students via an answer sheet

MATERIALS:

1) Newspaper or magazine pictures of modes of transportation.

2) Prepared cards with appropriate questions for the mode of transportation. Some sample questions for a picture of a ricksha are:

Name this mode of transportation. (picture of a man pulling a ricksha)
After you have found the entry, where does it tell you to look? (jinrikisha)
In what countries was this vehicle once widely used? (China and Japan)
Who once pulled these vehicles? (man)
Why were they declared illegal? (authorities felt using "human horses" was undignified)
Name the encyclopedia and volume used. [*World Book Encyclopedia* (1976), vol. 11 (J-K)]
Have you ever ridden in one?

On the back of each card, in the lower right-hand corner, place a letter (A-Z); these letters should correspond to those on the answer sheet.

3) Dry-mount the picture and the questions on a 6x9-inch oak-tag sheet with the picture at the top.

4) Master list of questions and answers dry-mounted to pieces of colored posterboard. List the questions and answers according to the letter on the oak-tag sheets (see materials 2).

5) Pencils and paper.

6) Large manila envelope (12x15-inches) for the materials.

PROCEDURE:

1) Two teams are formed by counting off in twos, but each student plays as an individual.

2) Place the oak-tag sheets face down on a table.

3) Make it clear that the questions are to be answered accurately.

4) Each player chooses a sheet, decides what the mode of transportation is, and chooses an encyclopedia to answer the questions.

5) Both accuracy and speed count toward overall team points. One point is awarded for each correct answer. Students should complete as many sheets as possible in the time allowed.

6) The prepared answer sheets may be used in one of two ways: an impartial student may check the answers as they are finished, or answers may be checked by the media specialist and reported back to the students.

* * *

```
****************************************************************
```
BUZZING THE Readers' Guide to Periodical Literature
```
****************************************************************
```

PURPOSE: To promote skill in the use of indexes to locate specific information.

GRADE LEVEL: 7th or 8th grade

TIME: 15-20 minutes per puzzle

NUMBER: Small group to an entire class

METHOD OF CHECKING: Answer sheet

MATERIALS:

1) Photocopies of pages from the *Abbreviated Readers' Guide to Periodical Literature* or the *Readers' Guide to Periodical Literature*; dry-mounted to a piece of colored posterboard. On the back, draw various irregular shapes in preparation for jigsaw puzzle-type cutting. Give each index page a number, then number each cut-out shape as belonging to one puzzle. Laminate and then cut out the pages into various pieces to make the jigsaw puzzle.

2) 10x13-inch manila envelopes to keep the puzzle pieces in; each envelope should be marked with the particular *Readers' Guide* used and the page number. In the lower right-hand corner, place the number for that particular puzzle.

3) A 6x9-inch oak-tag card with directions and questions for each index puzzle. Number each card to correspond with a puzzle, then type or letter the information necessary for Buzzing the . . . . For example:

Notice that the volume of the periodical is indicated by a number, then a colon and the page number (s): STEW—"Bountiful beef provencal, il *McCalls* 107:199-200 Mr '80. You are quickly able to learn that beef provencal is a stew; that the article appears in *McCalls* in volume 107 on pages 199-200 of the March, 1980 issue, and it is illustrated.

Use this code to determine in which volume and magazine you will find the following:

Information on LOVE—"why lovers are sometimes petty, mean, bitchy, and snide when what they really mean is I love you." (*Glamour* 78:166-7 + F '80)

Janet Lowe's contribution to "Schools everyone loves." (*Education Digest* 45:36-8 F '80)

The location of LOUISIANA cooking. (see COOKING, AMERICAN)

(Sample questions from page 265 of *Readers' Guide* Jan. 25-Apr. 22, 1980.)

Solve this arithmetic problem using the *Readers' Guide* page:

Take the page number on which you will find information about DOLL houses "Miniaturia." (52)

Add the page on which you will find the article "Have Telescopes Will Travel" by John Dosson. (339-44)

Substract the page on which you will find information on DOGS (Food & Feeding), "Sensible Pet Nutrition." (144 +)

Multiply by the page number on which you will find DOLLMAKING, "Helen Kish: the Irish doll artist." (16-18) What is your answer? (3,952)

(Materials list continues on page 70)

If more than one page is mentioned, such as 339-44 or 16-18 +, take the lower of the two pages for the problem.

(Sample problem from cross-references appearing on page 139 of *Readers' Guide* Jan. 25-Apr. 22, 1980.)

4) 9x12-inch master sheet of questions and answers for each index page. Several problems and/or questions fit on one sheet.

5) Paper and pencils (pens) for each student.

6) An appropriately sized cardboard box or a large manila envelope (16x20-inches) for the materials.

PROCEDURE:

1) Give each player a manila envelope containing the puzzle pieces and direction card, pencil and paper.

2) The players put the puzzles together and answer the questions on the oak-tag card by using the completed puzzle.

3) When the player has finished answering the questions, he or she raises a hand to indicate so and the media specialist brings the master sheet for checking.

4) One point is scored for each correct answer.

5) When two puzzles have been successfully completed and questions answered, a player may help someone else who is having trouble.

* * *

UNLOCKING THE FILE

PURPOSE: To assist students in mastering the use of the vertical file.

GRADE LEVEL: 7th or 8th grade

TIME: 2 50-minute periods

NUMBER: 2 classes

METHOD OF CHECKING: Students via answer sheet

MATERIALS:

1) 100 3x5-inch index cards; 50 per class.

2) The vertical file.

3) Paper and pencils or pens for each student.

4) Master list for each letter of the vertical file; list the folders in order.

5) Master lists with questions, answers, and documentation.

6) Large manila envelope (12x15-inches) for the materials if they are to be saved for another use.

PROCEDURE:

1) Assign class members certain letters of the alphabet. They are then responsible for those letters in the vertical file.

2) Students go to the vertical file and bring back the letter to their working area.

3) In a systematic order, each player goes through the folders and makes up a series of questions and answers along with proper documentation (source and page number when possible); five is a good number.

4) When finished, the student raises a hand to indicate so, and the media specialist hands him or her the master list for that letter (see materials 4). The player then places the folders in correct order so that the letter may be returned to the vertical file.

5) To be accomplished in one of two ways: each student picks out two of his or her "best" questions and writes them on index cards; or, a committee of five is formed and all questions are given to them for selection of the "best" to be written on the cards. Cards should be numbered and the numbers should correspond with the master list. In either case, a master list of questions, answers, and sources is compiled.

6) Both classes perform procedures 1-5 in the first period. In the second period, the questions of class 1 are given to class 2 to answer along with the source, and vice versa.

7) The answers are checked by the class that made up the questions, and the results reported to the media specialist.

8) The class with the most correct answers wins some type of prize; to be determined by the media specialist.

9) Index cards and master lists may be retained by the media specialist to be used in a scavenger hunt later in the year or for whatever reason.

* * *

SCAVENGER THROUGH REFERENCES

PURPOSE: To familiarize students with the variety of reference tools a media center contains.

GRADE LEVEL: 7th or 8th grade

TIME: 25-30 minutes

NUMBER: 4-6 players per team

METHOD OF CHECKING: Answer sheet/media specialist

MATERIALS:

1) 1 timer.

2) 1 scavenger list per team containing questions on the various reference materials available. For example:

Find the title of a pamphlet or newspaper article on each of the following subjects:
a. Indians (American) _____
b. King Tut _____
c. Computers _____
d. Mental illness _____

Find 5 synonyms for the word "benign" _____
Source _____

Locate a magazine article on each of the following subjects:
a. Loneliness
   Article's title _____
   Magazine's title _____
b. Ku Klux Klan
   Article's title _____
   Date of the magazine _____
   Pages of the article in the magazine _____
c. Olympic Games (1980)
   Article's title _____
   Is the article illustrated? _____

Write down the title of a book the media center has under each of these topics:
a. Baseball _____
b. Death _____
c. Motorcycles _____
d. Transportation _____

What African countries border the Mediterranean Sea? _____
Source _____

What does ornithology mean? _____
Source _____

Name a filmstrip that the media center has on ENERGY. What is its call number?
Title _____
Call Number _____ Source _____

What is the zip code for Thornton, Colorado? _____
Source _____

What is the Spanish word for snail? _____

Source _____

What event involving Orson Wells happened on 30 October 1938? _____

Source _____

Who said, "Never put off till tomorrow what you can do today?"

Source _____

3) Master list of questions and answers dry-mounted to a piece of colored posterboard; laminate. List the questions according to the number of the scavenger list.

4) Pencils and scrap paper.

5) Large manila envelope (12x15-inches) for the materials.

PROCEDURE:

1) Divide the class into teams of 4-6 players each. Appoint a leader for each group.

2) Give each captain pencils, scrap paper, and a scavenger list.

3) Each team is to gather together to discuss the items, then members may separate to look for the information.

4) When the information is located, players should return to their captain for recording; captains should also participate in the search.

5) There should be no collaboration between players after the initial discussion.

6) Start the teams at different questions on the scavenger list to ensure that too many students are not trying to use the same source at the same time. For example, one team starts at number one, another at number five, and another at the last question and works backwards.

7) No two questions are to be answered from the same source.

8) All teams are to return to a central area in 30 minutes whether they have completed the list or not.

9) Set the timer for 30 minutes.

10) If a team finishes ahead of time, suggest free reading, centers, quiet talking, and so on until the timer rings.

11) At the end of 30 minutes call everyone together. Have the leaders exchange lists and grade each other during a general discussion of the items and answers. Collect the lists.

12) If a dispute arises over the source, ask for proof; students can be ingenious!

13) For each question answered correctly by the team finishing first, give two points. One point per question for each of the remaining teams.

14) The team with the highest number of points is the winner and perhaps a small prize can be given.

15) Variation: Instead of a scavenger list, make up a set of 3x5-inch cards for each team with a number in the lower right-hand corner to correspond to a master list. The team leader can hand out cards to the team members and record the answers on paper, making sure all parts are completed.

* * *

REFERENCE AUCTION

PURPOSE: To assist students in understanding the types of information that can be found within different types of reference books.

GRADE LEVEL: 8th grade

TIME: 30-45 minutes

NUMBER: 3 players per group

METHOD OF CHECKING: Self-checking

MATERIALS:

1) 50 3x5-inch index cards, or 5 cards per set, bearing questions and answers concerning reference works. For example:

    From what source did the following quotation come, "Children of yesterday, heirs of tomorrow"? (*Bartlett's Familiar Quotations*)

    In what book would one find the explanation of the story "Pollyanna"? (*The Reader's Encyclopedia of American Literature*)

    What does the geographical term "Puszeta" mean? (*Larouss Encyclopedia of World Geography*)

    When was basketball invented? (*Famous First Facts*)

    What is the source of this sage excerpt, "Government even in its best state, is but a necessary evil; in its worst state, an intolerable one"? (*The Quotation Dictionary*)

    What is the main theme behind *A Raisin in the Sun*? (*International Library of Negro Life and History*, vol. I)

    What was the real name of "Billy the Kid"? (*The Trivia Encyclopedia*)

    What is another word for quotation? (*Roget's Thesaurus*)

    What was the Marocchi I, made from 1900-1901? (*The Complete Encyclopedia of Motorcars*)

    Who is Ganymede? (*Who's Who in Greek and Roman Mythology*)

    What is "Zero orbit"? (*The New Illustrated Space Encyclopedia*)

    Why was Robert Ball Hughes famous in the art world? (*Sculpture in America*)

    What is Mirkwood? (*Dictionary of Mythical Places*)

    Explain the musical term "Ombra scene." (*Harvard Dictionary of Music*)

    What is a "joikie"? (*Funk & Wagnalls Standard Dictionary of Folklore: Mythology & Legend*)

    What does the "Curse of Scotland" mean? (*Brewer's Dictionary of Phrase and Fable*)

    How tall can the "Common Lousewort" grow? (*Hammond Nature Atlas of America*)

    What is a "coaxial circle"? (*Mathematics Dictionary*)

    In what issue of a magazine would you find an article on Cartier, Jacques? (*National Geographic Index* or *Readers' Guide to Periodical Literature*)

    What time period does *The Red Badge of Courage* by Stephen Crane cover? (*Masterpieces of World Literature in Digest Form*)

    Explain the "coasting trade." (*Family Encyclopedia of American History*)

What is the nickname for Alabama? (*Stories of the States*)

If definite sets are desired, number five cards either on the back or front (all with the same number).

2) 1 stop watch or 1 timer for each group.

3) 1 die per group.

4) Chart for recording groups — winners and losers.

5) Large manila envelope (12x15-inches) for the materials.

PROCEDURE:

1) Divide the students into groups of three players and appoint a questioner from each group.

2) Give each questioner a set of cards and 1 die.

3) The remaining two students roll the die to determine who starts the "bidding." The student with the highest score begins; thereafter, they alternate turns.

4) The object is to get the players to find the reference works in the least amount of time.

5) The questioner reads the question and the first player who starts the bidding might say: "I can find the reference work in 5 minutes."

6) The second player may counter: "I can find the reference in 3 minutes."

7) Each player counters with lower time figures until one player says: "Find the reference."

8) Set the timer for the amount of time decided upon.

9) The player thus challenged must find the answer to the question asked, in a reference work, within the time limit set.

10) When the player finds the answer in a reference, he or she brings the work to the questioner for checking. If the answer is correct, the player wins the "round." If incorrect, the round is a forfeit, and no one wins.

11) Players continue to bid and find answers in reference works until one player, in each group, wins 3 out of 5 "rounds," thus winning the "match."

12) The winner of one group is then pitted against the winner of another group, and the loser against loser until ultimately one player emerges as a "Grand Winner."

13) Work the questioner into the game so that no one is left out.

* * *

ASSEMBLY LINE

PURPOSE: To teach the basic steps in running AV hardware and recognizing what AV software is used with the equipment.

GRADE LEVEL: 7th or 8th grade

TIME: 15-20 minutes per piece of equipment

NUMBER: 5 players per piece of equipment

METHOD OF CHECKING: Answer sheet and/or media specialist

MATERIALS:

1) 2 pieces of identical equipment for every 5 players such as: filmstrip projector, Dukane cassette sound filmstrip projector, opaque projector, and so on.

2) AV software that goes with the equipment used such as: filmstrip, filmstrip and cassette, book, map, and so on.

3) 3x5-inch index cards typed with one working step per card. At the top of each card, place the name of the piece of equipment to be used. If there is more than one loading process, as with the Dukane, indicate in the lower left-hand corner whether it is cassette or filmstrip loading. Each of the following directions would appear on its own card:

Dukane Sound Filmstrip Projector
Cassette loading:
Place projector on a firm stand or table.
Open compartment door by turning door knob to LEFT.
Insert cassette with openings at the top and tape supply on the right-hand side.
Snap cassette into place.

Filmstrip loading and framing:
Place projector on a firm stand or table.
Plug cord into electrical outlet.
Set power switch to the right of speaker to the LAMP position.
Remove film from its container and place in the curved, flexible holder on the inside of the door panel.
The START frame of the filmstrip should be extended out from the film holder towards the film receiver.
Insert the start of the filmstrip into the receiver below the arrows marked INSERT FILM. Be sure to push the filmstrip in all the way so that it engages in the first sprocket.
Hold the FILM CONTROL KEY down to the FAST FORWARD position until the "START" frame of the filmstrip appears on the screen.
If the film is not taken up automatically, gently guide it into the film receiver a little further while holding down the film key.
Using short downward taps on the film control key, advance the film until the first frame appears on the screen. Be careful only to TAP the film control key, because it responds very rapidly.
Close compartment door and turn knob to the RIGHT to latch.
To center the first frame on the viewing screen, turn the framing knob at the side of the unit until the frame is centered. If you have passed the first frame, press the film control key UPWARD to the REWIND position until you reach the first frame.

Using the focus knob, also at the side of the unit, FOCUS the picture.

To start the presentation, the first frame should be centered, focused, and in clear view of the audience.

To start the automatic presentation, push the cassette control PLAY button.

Adjust volume lever to a suitable sound level.

The filmstrip will automatically advance.

Thus, it will take twenty index cards to explain the cassette and filmstrip loading with another nine cards (steps) for finishing the presentation. Procedures for most pieces of equipment do not involve as many steps.

4) Extension cords where needed.

5) Screens or white butcher paper.

6) Answer sheets for each piece of equipment used which list the directions in a step-by-step logical sequence. Dry-mount each sheet to a piece of colored posterboard, then laminate.

7) Large manila envelope (16x20-inches) for the materials.

PROCEDURE:

1) Before the students arrive, scatter the equipment and extension cords (where needed) around the room. Two pieces of identical equipment per station.

2) Place the software to be used in a central location — several tables that have been placed together.

3) Divide the students into small groups of five. Choose a captain who will delegate authority.

4) Assign each team a station and hand them a pack of instruction cards that are mixed up.

5) Players must place the index cards in a logical sequential order.

6) When finished, the team leader raises a hand to indicate that the group is ready to be checked.

7) The media specialist can either check the cards or have the captain check them against the answer sheet. In the latter procedure, if something is incorrect, the captain must indicate so and become a bystander until the correction is made.

8) If all the cards are in correct order, the captain goes to the central tables and brings back the software to be used. If incorrect, work continues until all cards are in order.

9) The team now goes through the cards step-by-step to load the machines and demonstrate that they have "mastered" the technique.

10) When a piece of equipment has been "mastered," the team moves on to another set of machines, and begins again.

11) The team with the most demonstrations wins, or point values can be given for the difficulty of equipment.

12) The media specialist should circulate around the room to assist with any questions as to how to work any piece of equipment.

* * *

****

ANCIENT ARTIFACTS

****

PURPOSE: To provide practice in the operation of AV hardware through "hands on" experience.

GRADE LEVEL: 7th or 8th grade

TIME: 40-60 minutes

NUMBER: 3-4 players per piece of equipment

METHOD OF CHECKING: Media specialist and/or students

MATERIALS:

1) 1 piece of equipment for every 3-4 players, such as a film loop projector, 16mm movie projector, filmstrip projector, overhead projector, opaque projector, Dukane projector, language master, reel-to-reel tape recorder, slide projector, and so on. (The easier pieces of equipment, such as a cassette recorder and record player, were omitted since most students are already familiar with these.)

2) Instruction sheets for all pieces of equipment to be used.

3) AV software that goes with the equipment used, such as a film loop, 16mm film, filmstrip, transparency, book or map, filmstrip and cassette or record, audio flash cards, reel of audio tape, and slides, if the above equipment is selected.

4) Extension cords, screens and/or white butcher paper.

5) Scrap paper and pencils for each group.

6) Dittoed sheets with such questions as:

What is the item you are working with? How do you know?
What was the item's probable use?
What does the item imply about the society that used it?
Tell about the society.
After you have pieced together the society that developed the item you are examining demonstrate the ability to use their technology and explain why the equipment and software is used in the manner you suggest.

7) 1 timer.

PROCEDURE:

1) Before the students arrive, scatter the equipment, software, instruction sheets, and extension cords (where needed) around the room.

2) Divide the students into small groups of 3-4; choose a leader who also acts as a recorder.

3) Explain to the groups that they are archeologists who have discovered these artifacts from an unknown civilization. What can they deduce about the society from these clues?

4) Each recorder is to fill in a dittoed sheet; to be presented to the entire class later as the group report.

5) Assign the groups a piece of equipment and related materials.

6) Set the timer for a reasonable working period, leaving enough time at the end for the archaeological reports and demonstrations. Another period may be necessary for everyone to have a chance.

7) The media specialist should circulate around the room talking to the groups while they are working; asking such questions as, "How do you know that is a movie projector and was used for recording events? Maybe it was a weapon, or a toy, or a religious artifact." The media specialist should assist with any questions as to how to work any piece of equipment.

8) Have the students present their reports and demonstrations.

* * *

EXPRESSING THE MIND: LANGUAGE ARTS

ARE YOU LISTENING?

PURPOSE: To develop skill in listening to directions.

GRADE LEVEL: 7th or 8th grade

TIME: 30 minutes

NUMBER: 1 student to an entire class

METHOD OF CHECKING: Answer sheet

MATERIALS:
1) Cassette tape recorder and blank tape.
2) Pencils and paper.
3) Answer sheet dry-mounted to a piece of colored posterboard.
4) Stopwatch, clock, or watch with a second hand.

PROCEDURE:
1) This game can be given orally to the entire class, but is more effective for individuals or small groups of students, if tape recorded.
2) Directions:

   Place your name on the first line of the paper. On the third line write the numbers 1-10 across the page. Skip two lines and write the numbers across the page again. Do this until there are 10 rows of the numbers. For example:

   Name:

   1 2 3 4 5 6 7 8 9 10
   1 2 3 4 5 6 7 8 9 10
   1 2 3 4 5 6 7 8 9 10

(The example may also be dittoed to save time.)

Put your pencil down and listen to the directions before doing them. You will have 1 minute to complete the directions. Do not start until I say go.

   a) For the first line, put a check mark above 3, circle 6, and draw a square around the 9. Go (pause 1 minute).
   b) Put your pencil down and listen to directions for line 2:
   Under line 2, put a triangle above the 5, cross out 8, and circle 10. Go (pause 1 minute).
   c) Put your pencil down and listen to directions for line 3: Put a square between 3 and 4, a line above 6, a triangle under 8 and cross out 9. Go (pause 1 minute).
   d) Put your pencil down and listen to directions for line 4: Put the letter A between 1 and 2, draw a line under 4, circle 7, put a check mark over 8 and underline 10. Go (pause 1 minute).
   e) Put your pencil down and listen to directions for line 5: Draw a square around the 3, a triangle around the 7, put a check mark between 8 and 9, and cross out 10. Go (pause 1 minute).
   f) Put your pencil down and listen to directions for line 6: Circle 8, put a triangle above 3, underline 1 and 2, put a square above 10, and put a check mark under 5. Go (pause 1 minute).
   g) Put your pencil down and listen to the directions for line 7: Draw a checkmark above 10, circle 3, put an A above 5, put an X under 7 and circle 1. Go (pause 1 minute).

(Procedures continue on page 84)

h) Put your pencil down and listen to directions for line 8: Put a square above 5, put an X between 7 and 8, circle 3, put a triangle around 6, and put a check mark over 2. Go (pause 1 minute).

i) Put your pencil down and listen to the directions for line 9: Put a Z between 7 and 8, a box around 6, circle 5, put a triangle above 2, and cross out 9. Go (pause 1 minute).

j) Put your pencil down and listen to the directions for line 10: Put a triangle under 5, a square around 9, put a check mark above 1, put a triangle around 7, put a circle above 4, and a check mark over 1.

3) Players either rewind the tape and play it again to check their papers or use the answer sheet. If given orally, the teacher may read the answer sheet.

4) Each player recieves 1 point for each correct answer. The player with the highest score wins.

* * *

****
SPELLING ROCK
****

PURPOSE: To let students have fun while practicing spelling words.

GRADE LEVEL: 7th grade

TIME: 30 minutes

NUMBER: Entire class

METHOD OF CHECKING: Teacher

MATERIALS:

1) List of spelling words:

acquaintance	legible
advantageous	medieval
amateur	ninth
anxiety	paralysis
argue	questionnaire
bureau	rhythm
calendar	seize
caricature	siege
catastrophe	subtle
consensus	surprise
descent	tragedy
despair	twelfth
eligible	vacuum
fatigue	vengeance
heroes	weird

2) Pencil and paper or chalkboard for scorekeeping.

PROCEDURE:

1) The group is divided into two teams and arranged on two sides of the room as if the group were having a spelling bee.

2) The teacher determines which team is first and gives directions for the first round. Example, "For each 'a' in a word, you must not say 'a.' You must snap your fingers. For each 'e' you must turn in place." And so on.

3) Words are given to each team as if it were a spelling bee except a correct spelling (with appropriate actions) scores a point for the team and an incorrect spelling does not cause a player to sit out the remainder of the game.

4) After each round, different directions may be added. For example: "Shake a leg for a 't,' touch your left elbow for an 's,' and so on.

5) After 30 minutes of play, the team with the most points wins.

* * *

****
HUMAN FLY
****

PURPOSE: To provide practice in spelling.

GRADE LEVEL: 7th or 8th grade

TIME: 40 minutes

NUMBER: 2 players per gameboard

METHOD OF CHECKING: Self-checking

MATERIALS:

1) A Human Fly gameboard made from 14x22-inch colored posterboard.

2) 2 markers; little rubber spiders make good ones.

3) 35 3x4-inch colored posterboard cards bearing spelling words. Some examples are:

accommodate	calendar	interpreted
achievement	cemetery	knowledge
aggravate	compelled	maintenance
amateur	conscientious	misspell
apologize	different	opportunity
appetite	disappear	phenomenon
assistant	dissatisfied	prejudice
auxiliary	efficiency	repetition
barbarous	embarrass	subsequent
breathe	foreign	tragedy
brilliant	grammar	villain

The words were taken from the University of California's "List of Spelling Words Most Commonly Missed."

4) Five 3x4-inch posterboard cards bearing directions:

Rough surface—go down 1 story
Foot slipped—go down 1 story
Easy climb—go up 1 story
Smooth surface—go up 2 stories
Wet surface—go back to start

5) Answer sheet with correct spellings laminated to a piece of colored posterboard.

6) 1 die.

7) Manila envelope (16x20-inches) for materials.

PROCEDURE:

Form A

1) Players are given a Human Fly gameboard and related materials.

2) The spelling cards and direction cards are shuffled together and placed face down in a pile on the gameboard in the appropriate space.

3) The die is rolled to determine the order of play, and markers are placed at start.

4) The first player's opponent draws a card and reads the word that the first player must spell orally. If the word is correctly spelled, no move is made. The answer sheet may be consulted for correct answers.

5) If a direction card is drawn, the first player must follow the directions given.

6) Play continues with players alternating turns.

7) The first player to reach the top wins.

Form B

Played the same as Form A except the players write the spelling words on a chalkboard or a piece of paper.

* * *

LANGO

PURPOSE: To provide practice in recognizing parts of speech.

GRADE LEVEL: 7th grade

TIME: 40 minutes

NUMBER: 4 to 16 students

METHOD OF CHECKING: Caller

MATERIALS:

1) 16 9x12-inch oak-tag Lango cards with parts of speech randomly placed:

L	A	N	G	O
VERB	PRONOUN	CONJUNCTION	ADJECTIVE	NOUN
ADVERB	NOUN	PRONOUN	VERB	ADVERB
PRONOUN	PREPOSITION	FREE	PRONOUN	INTERJECTION
NOUN	CONJUNCTION	VERB	PREPOSITION	ADJECTIVE
ADJECTIVE	ADVERB	ADVERB	NOUN	CONJUNCTION

2) Master list for caller to mark words called, laminated to a piece of colored posterboard.

3) 40 3x4-inch colored posterboard cards bearing sentences with a word or words underlined. For example:

A wall of solid <u>brick</u> blocked our escape. (n.)
Last month <u>my</u> sister earned money for baby sitting. (pro.)
Sit down and <u>make</u> a list of the fifty states. (v.)
We ran <u>from</u> the old house with the tall windows and the wide porches. (prep.)
<u>Oh</u>! Have you ever seen an oil well? (interj.)
Her mother <u>disapproved</u> of her attitude. (v.)
The <u>activity</u> was publicized on television. (n.)
It was unusually cool <u>and</u> wet for August. (conj.)

The children weren't <u>suitably</u> dressed for winter. (adv.)
The motor <u>sounded</u> sluggish. (v.)
<u>Their</u> best player was ill. (pro.)
Jamie was the most attractive girl <u>in</u> the class. (prep.)
It was thoughtful of you to send <u>flowers</u>. (n.)
<u>We</u> are going to the museum Monday. (pro.)
Susan is ready <u>for</u> the dance. (prep.)
No one was aware of <u>the</u> news. (adj.)
Are <u>you</u> ready for the question. (pro.)
Which <u>comedy</u> shows do you enjoy most? (n.)
The stray cat <u>scratched</u> me. (v.)
The story was written by a friend of <u>mine</u>. (pro.)
Carol <u>and</u> Jim did not attend the meeting. (conj.)
<u>Well</u>, Dr. Johnson has moved into new offices. (interj.)
The crops were harvested <u>before</u> the first frost. (prep.)
George <u>wrote</u> that report. (v.)
June lives on a <u>ranch</u> in Texas. (n.)
He wanted to go to school <u>early</u>. (adv.)
The truck was stolen <u>during</u> the night. (prep.)
Dad chopped the <u>dry</u> wood for the fire. (adj.)
The award <u>was given</u> to Helen. (v.)
The family built a <u>new</u> house. (adj.)
Last week I swam <u>two</u> miles. (adj.)
He was careful <u>as</u> he crossed the street. (conj.)
The sailor was <u>happy</u> to leave the ship. (adj.)
Carelessness <u>causes</u> accidents. (v.)
<u>Margaret</u> looks like her mother. (n.)
All the boys <u>really</u> enjoy camping. (adv.)
The couple signed the <u>contract</u>. (n.)
My mother has been president <u>of</u> her club. (prep.)
The stone <u>is</u> an emerald. (v.)
<u>Our</u> family lived in Mexico. (pro.)

4) 16 6x9-inch manila envelopes with 20 plastic chips per envelope.

5) 40 plastic chips for the master list.

6) Large manila envelope (16x20-inches) for the materials.

PROCEDURE:

1) The game is played like Bingo, with caller taking the place of the teacher. Students choose a caller.

2) The caller draws a card, reads the sentence, repeating the underlined word, and asks a player to identify the part of speech underlined. If the answer is correct all players put a marker on that part of speech. If incorrect, the caller gives the correct answer and players put a marker on that part of speech.

3) Variation: The caller gives the column and the sentence and repeats the underlined word. Players must determine the part of speech and mark the cards accordingly without giving the answer orally.

* * *

STAR FLIGHT

PURPOSE: To expand vocabularies by assimilation of some Greek and Latin prefixes, suffixes, and root words.

GRADE LEVEL: 8th grade

TIME: 30 minutes

NUMBER: 4 players per gameboard

METHOD OF CHECKING: Answer sheet

MATERIALS:

1)   1 Star Flight gameboard made from 14x22-inch colored posterboard.

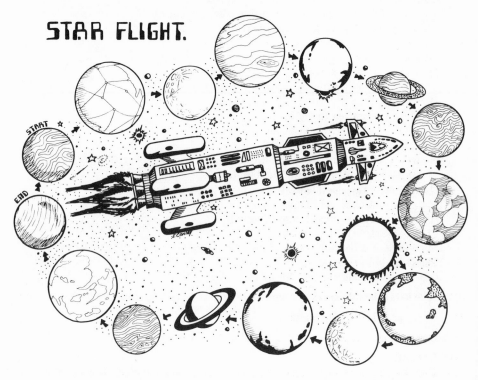

STAR FLIGHT.

2)   4 markers per gameboard.

3)   4 Help cards (3x5-inch index cards) each bearing the following lists:

Greek

Prefix	Root	Suffix
anti (against)	dem (people)	cracy (rule)
hyper (over)	geo (earth)	ism (condition of being)
micro (small)	hydro (water)	ist (one who)
peri (around)	meter (measure)	mania (madness for)
tele (for)	therm (heat)	phobia (dread of)

	Latin	
Prefix	**Root**	**Suffix**
con (with)	aud (hear)	able, ible (capable of)
ex (out)	cred (believe)	er, ir (one who)
in (not)	vert (turn)	ous (full of)
pre (before)	vid, vis (see)	tion, sion (act of)
re (again)	voc (call)	ty (state or quality)

4) 1 die.

5) 30 3x4-inch colored posterboard cards bearing:

convert	invisible
divert	monopolist
aversion	audition
evident	hydrophobia
vision	conversion
television	juror
vocal	elevator
evoke	thermometer
provoke	reversible
revoke	socialism
periscope	creation
perimeter	activity
preclude	furious
antitoxin	credit
prevent	tolerable

6) Answer sheet dry-mounted to a piece of colored posterboard.

7) Large manila envelope (16x20-inches) for the materials.

PROCEDURE:

1) Players are given a Star Flight gameboard and related materials.

2) Cards are shuffled and placed face down in the center of the gameboard on the spaceship. Markers are placed on Start and players are each given a Help card. The die is rolled to determine order of play.

3) The first player draws a card, reads the word aloud and decides whether or not to use the Help card to determine the meaning of the word. If the Help card is used in giving the definition the player moves one planet on the gameboard after giving a correct answer.

4) If the Help card is not used and the player gives a correct definition, the die is rolled and the player moves the number of spaces indicated by the die. The card is placed at the bottom of the pile in either case.

5) Other players may check correct answers by consulting the answer sheet.

6) If the definition given is not correct the player stays on the same planet.

7) Play continues with players alternating turns.

8) The first player to reach End wins.

* * *

****
PYRAMID PROBE
****

PURPOSE: To promote skillful use of capitalization.

GRADE LEVEL: 7th or 8th grade

TIME: 40 minutes

NUMBER: 2-4 players per gameboard

METHOD OF CHECKING: Answer sheet

MATERIALS:

1) Pyramid Probe gameboard made from 14x22-inch colored posterboard.

2) 4 markers per gameboard.

3) 20 3x4-inch colored posterboard cards bearing sentences in all little letters. For example:

i went to chruch on easter sunday.
the apache was friendly to me.
according to him, the show is sold out.
i live on elm street.
carol visited her aunt in chicago.
have you read *bel ria*?
the new machines are being tested.
have you visited yellowstone park?
many visitors were expected this year.

albany is the capital of the state of new york.
eskimos live near the arctic circle.
what is the correct time?
mrs. smith smiled as she walked across the room.
rosalie mailed the package.
mr. williams preferred to play football.
"if you need help," said warren, "call me."
you should turn south at the corner.
we traveled through the northwest.
denver is the capital of colorado.
jose finished his work.

4) Master list of sentences laminated to a piece of colored posterboard.

5) Large manila envelope (16x20-inches) for the materials.

PROCEDURE:

1) Players are given a Pyramid Probe gameboard and related materials.

2) Players determine the order of play and place their markers at Start.

3) The first player shuffles the cards, places them on the gameboard and draws a card. The player reads the sentence and identifies the word or words that should be captialized.

4) An opposing player may check the answer sheet to verify an answer.

5) If correct, the player moves the marker to the first space containing the same number as are capital letters in the sentence. For example: "the apache was friendly to me." The example contains two words that should begin with capital letters—The and Apache. Therefore, the player moves to the first space marked 2. The card is placed at the bottom of the pile.

6) If the player is incorrect, the marker is not moved.

7) If a player lands on a space that is occupied, the first marker occupying the space is sent back to start.

8) The game continues in this fashion with players alternating turns.

9) The winner is the first player to reach finish.

* * *

STAR BATTLES

PURPOSE: To provide practice in the use of commas.

GRADE LEVEL: 7th or 8th grade

TIME: 40 minutes

NUMBER: 2 students per gameboard

METHOD OF CHECKING: Answer sheet

MATERIALS:

1) 1 checkerboard for every two students.

2) Star Battles ships (*see* diagrams on page 95).

Red	**Black**
4 Starfighter warships	4 Starfighter warships
8 Starprobe scout ships	8 Starprobe scout ships

3) 32 Star Battles cards of 3x4-inch colored posterboard bearing sentences from the answer sheet with the commas left out.

4) Answer sheet laminated to a piece of colored posterboard. Example sentences:

Commas in a series:
a) Men, women, and children crowded around the airplane.
b) Mrs. Williams, her sister, and I went to lunch.
c) The boys ate lunch, played frisbee, and watched television.
d) We finished the popcorn, peanuts, and potato chips.
e) Sam changed the oil, greased the chasis, and rotated the tires.
f) Take out the garbage, sweep the porch, and go to the store.
g) The students reviewed the chapter, studied notes, and took a test.
h) Will you call Mary, make plans, and ask her to bring the meat?

Commas to set off an appositive:
a) My sister, Mrs. Principate, loves animals.
b) My new teacher, Miss Grey, gave us homework.
c) Denver, the capital of Colorado, has a dry climate.
d) The book, *My Shadow Ran Fast*, is good reading.
e) His dog, Schnapps, was not a good hunting dog.
f) Mr. Mead, the flight instructor, gave the check rides.
g) Will you invite the new girl, Susan Hunter?
h) The music director, Walter Rhodes, did a good job with the students.

Commas after introductory words:
a) Yes, I plan to go to the movie.
b) Oh, she didn't answer the telephone.
c) No, I haven't the faintest idea when he'll be home.
d) Yes, you may go.
e) Oh, did you buy the present?
f) No, flying is too dangerous.
g) Yes, we are pleased with the service.
h) Golly, she was rude!

Commas after introductory dependent clauses:
a) Without Mother, Bill wouldn't know what to do.
b) After the fire, the weary men slept for hours.
c) According to my grandfather, the treasure was buried.

(Materials list continues on page 96)

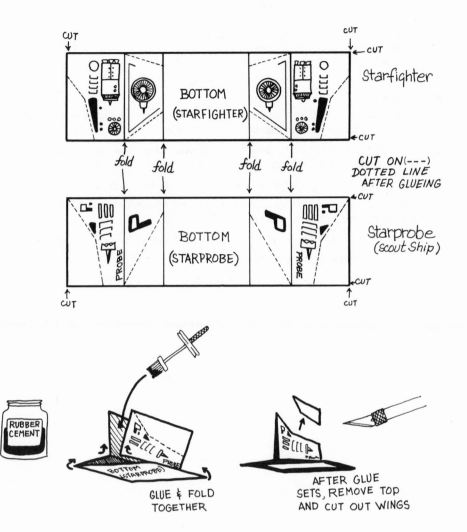

Starfighter

BOTTOM (STARFIGHTER)

CUT ON (---) DOTTED LINE AFTER GLUEING

Starprobe (scout Ship)

BOTTOM (STARPROBE)

RUBBER CEMENT

GLUE & FOLD TOGETHER

AFTER GLUE SETS, REMOVE TOP AND CUT OUT WINGS

COMPLETED PLAYING PIECE

      d) After the dance, the couple went out for a hamburger.

      e) When the team won, the crowd roared with approval.

      f) Before the game, the players tried to stay calm.

      g) When Helen left, the office was quiet.

      h) Because of the money situation, the work was stopped.

5)   Large manila envelope (16x20-inches) for the materials.

PROCEDURE:

1)   Players are given a checkerboard, Star Battles ships, and cards. Determine order of play, and arrange ships on the board as in checkers.

2)   The beginning player draws a card and indicates where commas should be placed. The opposing player may use the answer sheet to check for correct answers.

3)   If correct, a ship is moved one space. If incorrect, no moves are made.

4)   Players take turns answering, moving a ship each turn with the objective of capturing the opposing ships by jumping (as in checkers).

5)   The warships may be moved one space in any direction for each correct answer.

6)   The scout ships may only be moved one space forward for each correct answer.

7)   The first player to capture the opponents' warships wins.

* * *

****

QUOTATION ROCK

****

PURPOSE: To develop skill in the use of quotation marks.

GRADE LEVEL: 7th or 8th grade

TIME: 30 minutes

NUMBER: 2-4 players per gameboard

METHOD OF CHECKING: Answer key

MATERIALS:

1) Quotation Rock gameboard made from 14x22-inch colored posterboard.

2) 4 markers per gameboard.

3) 1 die.

4) 28 3x4-inch colored posterboard cards each bearing one of the sentences on the answer key but without the quotation marks. (Include the number of the sentence as it appears on the answer key for ease in checking.)

5) Answer key, dry-mounted to a piece of colored posterboard. Some examples are:

"Come with me," said Susan.
"Lois always says, 'I'm not sure,'" remarked Sam.
Tom said, "Let's go to the beach."
"Yes, you are correct," he replied.
Mr. Landers said that the rain began to fall at one o'clock.

(Materials list continues on page 98)

Did you read the chapter entitled, "Airplane Instruments"?
"Are you going to buy that dress?" asked Ann.
"No," said Carol. "My mother doesn't like it."
"Everytime we want to swim," Andrew complained, "it rains."
The cashier said that all the tickets were sold.
"It can't be true!" exclaimed Don.
"We've been wanting to see that movie for a long time," said Carol.
My favorite painting is the "Mona Lisa."
Miss Young said that she was afraid of flying in an airplane.
"Your books are on the table," said mother.
"I'm glad that you reminded me," said Bill.
"If I had forgotten those books, I would be in trouble," he replied.
June said that we could receive a free prize with the coupon.
I didn't enjoy the chapter entitled "Socialism."
The newsman said that 10 people were killed in a plane crash.
Allen suggested, "We could play baseball."
"I'm sure," he said, "that the papers were left on the desk."
"I want to go home," remarked the boy. "I didn't mean to cause any trouble."
Kim asked if she traveled a great deal each year.
She said that when she falls she is embarrassed.
"All of us are doing what we can," said Allen.
"Yes, you are correct," he replied.
The speech entitled "America, My Home" was excellent.

6) 10 3x4-inch colored posterboard ♪ cards bearing directions:

Go back to start
Off-key, lose one turn
Good beat, move forward 1 space
Good rhythm, move forward 2 spaces
Now you're rocking, move forward 1 space
Rest, lose a turn
Wrong note, go back to start
Slow beat, move back 1 space
Lose 1 turn
Boogie, back to start

7) Large manila envelope (16x20-inches) for the materials.

PROCEDURE:

1) Players are given a Quotation Rock gameboard and related materials.

2) Cards are shuffled and placed in the appropriate spaces on the gameboard.

3) Markers are placed on Start and players roll the die to determine the order of play.

4) The first player draws a card, reads the sentence, inserting quotation marks, and places the card at the bottom of the pile. If correct, the player rolls the die and moves the number of spaces indicated by the die. If incorrect, no move is made and the next player takes a turn. Correct answers may be verified by the use of the answer key.

5) Play continues with players alternating turns.

6) When a player lands on a ♪, a ♪ card is drawn and the directions must be followed.

7) The first player to reach the end is the winner.

* * *

****
KETTLE
****

PURPOSE: To help students identify and become familiar with verbs.

GRADE LEVEL: 7th grade

TIME: 30 minutes

NUMBER: 2 students

METHOD OF CHECKING: Self-checking

MATERIALS:
1) Pencils and paper.

PROCEDURE:
1) Players determine the order of play.

2) The first player writes a sentence on a piece of paper. The sentence is read aloud substituting "kettle" for the verb. For example: Allen kettle (ran) to the store.

3) The second player asks questions that can be answered yes or no, attempting to gain clues to the word. For example: "Is this something I can do?"

4) The second player must guess the verb after 12 questions in order to receive 10 points and gain a turn. If the verb is not guessed after 12 questions, the first player reads the sentence with the correct verb, receives 5 points and chooses another sentence.

5) The player with the highest score after 30 minutes of play wins.

* * *

RIDDLER

PURPOSE: To let students have fun with some parts of speech and synonyms.

GRADE LEVEL: 7th or 8th grade

TIME: 40 minutes

NUMBER: Form A: 4-16 players; Form B: entire class

METHOD OF CHECKING: Answer sheet

MATERIALS:

1)   2 Riddler Record boards made of 9x12-inch tagboard.

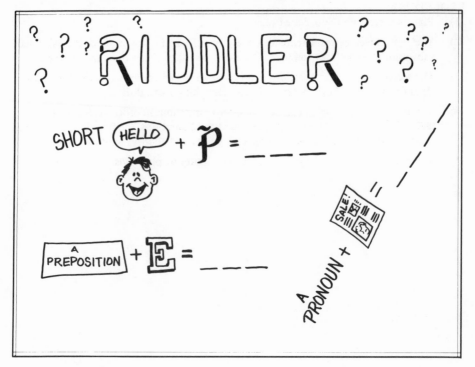

2)   2 Vis-A-Vis® pens.

3)   3 sheets each laminated to a piece of colored posterboard containing the following riddles (one with answers included, to be used as the answer sheet):

fast turn + e = (spine)
B + shower = (brain)
prep + r + adverb = (torso)
part of a fish + g + suffix = (finger)
be quiet + prep = (shin)
SK + prep = (skin)
used in golf + th = (teeth)
B + number = (bone)
article + K + le = (ankle)
payment + T = (feet)

e + L + ribbon = (elbow)
To listen + t = (heart)
negative + se = (nose)
to exist + r = (liver)
t + up = (thigh)
f + high card = (face)
e + biblical form of you = (eye)
h + what you breathe = (hair)
n + to be ill = (nail)
a prep + e = (toe)
h + a conjunction = (hand)
short hello + p = (hip)

4) Dictionaries, English books or other materials.

5) Damp paper towels.

6) Large manila envelope (16x20-inches) for the materials.

PROCEDURE:

Form A

1) The group is divided into two teams with each team choosing a captain.

2) The captains are given Riddler Record boards, Vis-A-Vis® pens, and riddle sheets.

3) The teacher retains the answer sheet until the end of the game and gives the clue that all riddles relate to parts of the body.

4) The team players work together to solve the riddles, using the dictionaries, English books, or other materials.

5) When an answer is discovered, the captain records it on the Riddler Record board.

6) When a team finishes, or time is called, the records are checked with the answer sheet.

7) The team with the most correct answers wins.

Form B

Played the same as Form A except players each have a Riddler Record board and Vis-A-Vis® pen and play as individuals. The player with the most correct answers wins.

* * *

DREAM MACHINES

PURPOSE: To provide practice in standard usage of English.

GRADE LEVEL: 7th or 8th grade

TIME: 40 minutes

NUMBER: 2-4 players per gameboard

METHOD OF CHECKING: Answer sheet

MATERIALS:

1) A Dream Machines gameboard made from 14x22-inch colored posterboard.

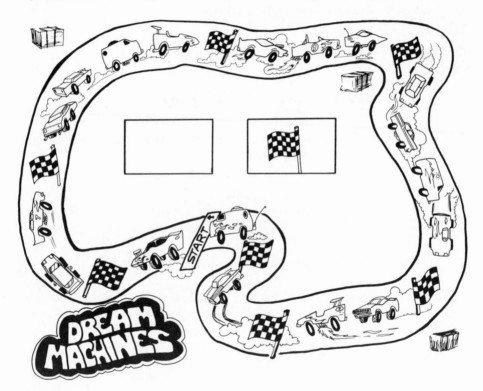

2) 4 markers.

3) 2 dice.

4) 10 3x4-inch Flag cards bearing the following directions:

    Out of gas, lose one turn
    Clear freeway, take another turn
    Caught speeding, go back 3 spaces
    Flat tire, miss one turn
    Bad accident, go back to start
    Slow traffic, lose next turn
    Good mileage, move ahead 1 space
    Long train, go back 1 space

Rough road, go back 3 spaces
Good driving, move ahead 2 spaces

5) 20 3x4-inch colored posterboard Question cards bearing sentences with grammatical errors, numbered to correspond to the answer sheet.

6) Answer sheet laminated to a piece of colored posterboard. Sample sentences:

I *ain't* going to finish it. (am not)
Janice and *him* are going to the dance. (he)
They're skiis were left outside the lodge. (their)
Why *don't* the teacher explain the assignment? (doesn't)
I had never *sang* that song. (sung)
Her and me are going on a hike. (She and I)
Which is *tallest*, an elephant or a giraffe? (taller)
Have you *spoke* to your family about the party? (spoken)
Have you *rode* the roller coaster, yet? (ridden)
Dad has never *broke* a promise. (broken)
The flowers smell *sweetly*. (sweet)
Sam was hurt *bad* in the accident. (badly)
You should *of* seen me win the contest. (have)
That meat smells *badly* to me. (bad)
Carol plays the violin *good*. (well)
Miss James hopes that nobody forgets *their* lines. (his) (her)
My feet were nearly *froze* after ice skating. (frozen)
Mom sent Joel and *I* for some hamburgers. (me)
We *seen* the concert last week. (saw)
The girls worked *good* together. (well)

7) Large manila envelope (16x20-inches) for the materials.

PROCEDURE:

1) Players are given the Dream Machines gameboard, dice, Flag cards, markers and Question cards. The Flag and Question cards are placed face down in a pile on the appropriate area as marked on the gameboard, markers are placed on Start, and players roll the dice to determine the order of play.

2) The first player rolls the dice, draws a Question card and identifies and corrects the error shown on the card. If correct, the player moves the marker the number of spaces indicated on the dice and places the Question card at the bottom of the pile. If incorrect, the next player takes a turn.

3) If a player lands on a Flag, a Flag card is drawn; the player follows the directions on the card and places the card at the bottom of the pile.

4) Players continue to alternate turns. The first player to reach Start after circling the board wins.

* * *

KINGS AND QUEENS

PURPOSE: To help students recognize simple sentences and sentence fragments.

GRADE LEVEL: 7th or 8th grade

TIME: 30 minutes

NUMBER: 4 students per gameboard

METHOD OF CHECKING: Answer sheet

MATERIALS:

1) 1 Kings and Queens gameboard for every 4 students. Gameboards can be made from posterboard.

2) 45 3x4-inch colored posterboard cards bearing sentence fragments, run-on sentences, and simple sentences. Number the cards as illustrated:

3) 9 3x4-inch spade cards bearing the following directions:

lose one turn	move ahead 3 spaces
go back 3 spaces	go back to start
move ahead 1 space	move ahead 2 spaces
lose a turn	go back 2 spaces
lose the next turn	

4) Master sheet laminated to a piece of colored posterboard. The following are sample sentences:

Simple sentences:
a) Shut the door.
b) It was closed.
c) We're ready.
d) I was hiding.
e) The door was locked.
f) Someone snickered.
g) Poems can be funny.
h) Complete the application.
i) The telephone rang.
j) Some letters are critical.
k) Riddles are popular.
l) Exercise can be fun.
m) We were thirsty.
n) The classes hurried outdoors.
o) He was proud.

Sentence fragments:
a) Through that door.
b) The busiest man in the city.
c) Trying to keep the tears back.
d) Glancing at the paper.
e) An hour ago.
f) Raced up the stairs.
g) Knocked over the nails.
h) A city on the river.

(Materials list continues on page 106)

i) May be written.
j) Staring at each other.
k) Somewhere in the distance.
l) Trying to shake her hand.
m) What time?
n) The star of our parties.
o) Greg on their shoulders.

Run on sentences:
a) I got to the store late, it was closed.
b) John has been absent he has mumps.
c) The wind rose during the night, soon it was raining.
d) That boy is Bill Johnson, he lives across the street.
e) All the trees were cut down we miss them.
f) My sister likes music, she plays the piano.
g) Today is November 15, it is my birthday.
h) The dog barked, everyone listened.
i) The class could not get out, the door was locked.
j) I want to go downtown I need a book.
k) George collects stamps Sue collects dolls.
l) We were watching a man, he had a blue car.
m) Two girls in our class have been absent they have the flu.
n) That is Carol Lee she lives next door.
o) We left for the mountains, he stayed home.

5)   4 markers per gameboard.

6)   Large manila envelope (16x20-inches) for the materials.

PROCEDURE:

1)   Players are given a Kings and Queens gameboard, markers, and cards.

2)   The sentence cards are shuffled and placed face down in the middle of the board. Each player draws a card to determine the order of play. HIgh card gets first turn.

3)   The sentence cards are re-shuffled, the spade cards are shuffled and both sets of cards are placed face down in a pile in the middle of the board in the appropriate space.

4)   Players place markers at Start.

5)   The first player draws a card, reads it aloud, and identifies it as a simple sentence, sentence fragment, or run-on sentence. The other players may check the answer sheet to see if the answer is correct.

6)   If correct, the player moves the number of spaces indicated on the card. If incorrect, the player does not move his or her marker. If a player lands on a spade, a spade card is drawn and the directions are followed.

7)   Play continues in this manner with players taking turns.

8)   The player who circles the board first wins.

* * *

```
*****************************************************************
```

SUPER HEROES

```
*****************************************************************
```

PURPOSE: To familiarize students with tall tale characters.

GRADE LEVEL: 7th or 8th grade

TIME: 30 minutes

NUMBER: 2-4 students per pack of cards

METHOD OF CHECKING: Self-checking

MATERIALS:

1) 32 3x4-inch color posterboard cards per pack. Each pair consists of a name and a description of a tall tale character. For example:

<table>
<tr>
<td>

SUPERMAN

</td>
<td>

He flies as fast as a speeding bullet and can leap tall buildings in a single bound.

</td>
</tr>
</table>

Pecos Bill	Old Stormalong
Davy Crockett	John Henry
Johnny Appleseed	Sam Patch
Paul Bunyan	Joe Magarac
Bionic Woman	Annie Oakley
Incredible Hulk	Bat Man
Robin	Superman
Wonder Woman	Spiderman

2) Large manila envelope (10x13-inches) for the materials.

PROCEDURE:

1) Players determine the order of play.

2) The first player shuffles the cards and places them face down on the table. The cards are laid out in any pattern, but no two cards should touch each other.

3) Each player will want to remember the position of each card as it is turned up on the table, since this will help in building pairs.

4) The first player begins the game by turning up any two cards, one at a time. All players look at the two cards as they are turned up, but the two cards are not immediately picked up, just turned face up.

5) If the two cards are a pair, the player picks them up, keeps them, and turns up two more cards. The player's turn continues as long as he or she continues to turn up pairs.

(Procedures continue on page 108)

6) If the two cards are not a pair, they are turned face down again and left in thei original places. This ends the first player's turn. (Cards are picked up only when the: are a pair.)

7) Play continues in this manner with players taking turns.

8) The winner is the player who has accumulated the greatest number of pairs after all the cards have been picked up from the table.

* * *

MR. ZB3

PURPOSE: To test reading comprehension.

GRADE LEVEL: 7th or 8th grade

TIME: 40 minutes

NUMBER: 4 students per gameboard

METHOD OF CHECKING: Self-checking

MATERIALS:

1) 1 Mr. ZB3 gameboard for every 4 students playing. Gameboards can be made from 14x22-inch colored posterboard.

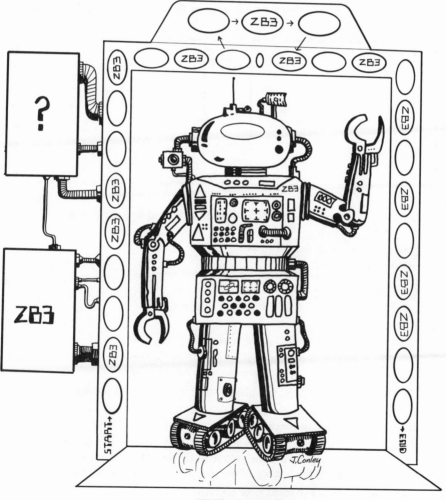

MR.ZB3

(Materials list continues on page 110)

2)   4 markers per gameboard.

3)   1 spinner.

4)   30 3x4-inch colored posterboard cards bearing questions such as:

In what state did *Caddie Woodlawn* take place?
Why did Caddie warn the Indians of the impending attack by the men of Dunnville?
What did Tom and Caddie put on exhibit?
Who saved the school house from fire?
How did Tom and Caddie treat Annebelle when she arrived?
In what period of time is *Johnny Tremain* set?
How could one tell if Johnny was angry?
In what field was Johnny an apprentice?
What happens to Johnny to cause him to become a dispatch rider?
What part did Johnny play in the Boston Tea Party?

(Questions may be all from the same book or from several different books.)

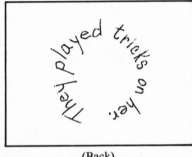

How did Tom and
Caddie treat
Annebelle when
she arrived?

(Front)   (Back)

5)   15 3x4-inch colored posterboard ZB3 cards bearing directions such as:

Short circuit — go back 2 spaces
Power surge — move ahead 1 space
Low power cell — lose 1 turn
Need reprogramming — lose next turn
Fresh batteries — move ahead 3 spaces

6)   Large manila envelope (16x20-inches) for the materials.

PROCEDURE:

1)   Players are given a Mr. ZB3 gameboard and related materials.

2)   Cards are shuffled. The question cards are placed face up and ZB3 cards are placed face down in piles on the appropriate spaces on the board.

3)   Markers are placed on Start and players spin the spinner to determine order of play.

4)   The first player draws a question card, reads the question aloud and answers the question. The answer is checked by reading the back of the card.

5)   If correct, the player spins the spinner, moves the number of spaces indicated by the spinner, and places the card at the bottom of the pile. If incorrect, no move is made, the card is placed at the bottom of the pile, and the next player takes a turn.

6)   Play continues with players alternating turns.

7)   When a player lands on a ZB3 space, a ZB3 card is drawn and directions must be followed.

8)   The first player to reach the end wins.

* * *

PARK IT!

PURPOSE: To train students to skim for information.

GRADE LEVEL: 7th or 8th grade

TIME: 40 minutes

NUMBER: 4 students per gameboard

METHOD OF CHECKING: Self-checking; answer sheet for teacher

MATERIALS:

1) 1 Park It! gameboard for every 4 students playing from 14x22-inch colored poster-board (*see* page 112).

2) 40 3x4-inch colored posterboard cards bearing questions. Some examples taken from the *Colorado Driver's Manual* are:

How is freeway driving different from driving on a regular street?
When parking downhill, how should wheels be turned?
Who has the right-of-way at uncontrolled intersections?
What is the left turn rule?
Does a motorized bicycle operator need a license?
What does a triangle represent?
What vehicles are required by law to stop at all railroad crossings?
Why are safety belts required?
What is the difference between white and yellow road markings?
What are five steps to follow if one is involved in an accident?
How many points are assessed for speeding?
For what reasons can a license be suspended, revoked, or cancelled?
What tests must one undergo in order to receive a driver's license?
There are several locations where it is forbidden to stop, stand, or park. What are these locations?
What is the speed limit in a business district?
What does a solid yellow line on the road indicate?
How many kinds of highway signs exist?
What is the procedure for entering a freeway?
What are the five steps in making a turn?

3) 20 3x4-inch colored posterboard penalty cards bearing:

Stop light — lose one turn
Bad accident — go back 2 spaces
Flat tire — go back 1 space
Out of gas — go back 2 spaces
Speeding — go back to start
Driving too slowly — go back 1 space
Mechanical trouble — go back 1 space
Improper turn — go back 2 spaces
Slow train — lose a turn
Dead end — lose a turn
School zone — go back 1 space
Blow-out — go back 3 spaces
Barricade — lose next turn
Road closed — lose a turn
Rough road — go back 2 spaces
Road repair — go back 1 space

(Materials list continues on page 113)

Stop sign—lose a turn
Ice on road—go back 1 space
Traffic jam—lose a turn
Slow traffic—go back 2 spaces

4) Stopwatch, watch, or clock with a second hand.

5) 4 copies of the state drivers' license manual per gameboard.

6) 4 markers per gameboard.

7) Answer sheet dry-mounted to a piece of colored posterboard.

8) Large manila envelope (16x20-inches) for the materials.

PROCEDURE:

1) Players are given a Park It! gameboard and related materials.

2) Cards are shuffled and placed in appropriate spaces on the gameboard, markers are placed on start, players determine order of play, and each player is given a drivers' license manual.

3) Player 1 draws a question card, reads the question aloud, and has one minute to skim through the manual to find the correct answer. The page number on which it is found and the correct answer are read aloud. Other players may check the answer with the manual and/or the answer sheet.

4) If correct, player 1 moves the same number of spaces as the number of the page bearing the correct answer. If the page has a double digit number, the player adds the digits together to determine the number of spaces to move. (If after adding the digits together, the sum is still a double digit, those digits are then added together.) Player 1 returns the card to the bottom of the pile.

5) If incorrect, no move is made and the card is returned to the bottom of the pile.

6) Players continue to play by alternating turns. When a player lands on a space containing a police car, a penalty card is drawn and directions are followed.

7) The first player to reach the parking zone wins.

* * *

DEDUCTION

PURPOSE: To promote proficiency in critical reading.

GRADE LEVEL: 7th or 8th grade

TIME: 25 minutes

NUMBER: 1 student per envelope

METHOD OF CHECKING: Self-checking

MATERIALS:

1) Brochures describing automobiles and motorcycles from automobile and motorcycle dealers. (Pictures and descriptions may also be taken from catalogs. Pictures, however, should have similar descriptions to allow for critical reading.)

2) 9x12-inch tagboard or posterboard for each group of puzzles.

3) Rubber cement.

4) 1 manila envelope (10x13-inches) for materials for each player.

PROCEDURE:

Preparation

1) Cut out the picture of the auto or motorcycle and the paragraph describing the item. (Approximately 5 pictures will be needed for 1 board with 2 extra pictures needed for dummy puzzle pieces.)

2) Glue the matching pictures and descriptions on the tagboard and cut them apart.

3) Include 4 extra pieces (2 pictures, 2 descriptions) that do not match.

Play

1) Two players are each given an envelope containing puzzle pieces.

2) The players race to match each picture with its description.

3) The puzzle is put together to check for successful critical reading.

4) The first player to finish the puzzle wins.

* * *

```
********************************************************************
```
COMPOUND THE WORDS
```
********************************************************************
```

PURPOSE: To reinforce the concept of compound and base words.

GRADE LEVEL: 7th or 8th grade

TIME: 20-25 minutes

NUMBER: 2-4 players per set

METHOD OF CHECKING: Self-checking

MATERIALS:
1) 38 dominoes made of 2x4-inch pieces of colored posterboard or 3x5-inch index cards. Each domino bears a compound or base word.

WILDCAT	CATTAIL	TAILGATE

Sample set:

wintergreen	greenwood	woodcut
bulkhead	headfirst	firsthand
housework	workbook	bookcase
bonefish	fisheye	eyecup
wildcat	cattail	tailgate
hereafter	afterworld	worldwide
houseboat	boathouse	housecarl
horseback	backfire	fireweed
policeman	manpower	powerhouse
cookbook	bookstore	storefront
world	bone	weed
fish	green	book
winter	horse	

If more than one set is desired, use different words.

2) Large manila envelope (12x15-inches) for the materials.

PROCEDURE:
1) Groups of 2-4 players are formed by counting off.

2) Each group sits at a table and is given a set of compound or base word dominoes.

3) The dominoes are shuffled and placed face down, and each player picks five dominoes.

4) If there are any dominoes left over, they are set aside as the boneyard.

5) Each player holds the dominoes so the other players can see only the backs of the dominoes.

6) The first player puts down a card, face up—the one with cattail on it, perhaps.

(Procedures continue on page 116)

7) The player to the left looks at his or her cards to see whether he or she has one that contains either base word, cat or tail. If the hand contains tailgate, it is placed next to the right side of cattail to block off the side of the dominoes that has tail on it.

8) The next player looks at his or her dominoes for a word with either cat or gate in it, the exposed base words. If he or she has wildcat, the domino can be played on the left of the cattail domino because the same base word will be next to each other.

9) Rules for playing a domino with a single baseword on it are the same as for any other domino.

10) If a player cannot match either exposed base word, dominoes should be drawn from the boneyard until a match is made. Those dominoes drawn are now part of the players hand.

11) If the player still cannot play after cleaning out the boneyard, the next player takes a turn.

12) The first player to use up his or her dominoes wins.

13) If none of the players can make a play and the boneyard dominoes are gone, the game ends in a block.

14) All the players count the dominoes held by each individual. The player with the fewest dominoes wins.

* * *

****

GODS & GODDESSES

****

PURPOSE: To promote an awareness of gods and goddesses of Greek mythology.

GRADE LEVEL: 7th or 8th grade

TIME: 30 minutes

NUMBER: 3-5 students per pack of cards

METHOD OF CHECKING: Self-checking

MATERIALS:

1) 12 "sets" of 4 (total 48) cards, approximately 2½x3½-inches, bearing names and pictures of Greek gods and goddesses. A set is 4 of the same card (4 Zeus, 4 Hermes, and so on).

(Materials list continues on page 118)

2)   Large manila envelope (12x15-inches) for the materials.

PROCEDURE:

1)   The cards are dealt, one at a time, until all cards are given out. The number of cards received is not important; some players may have more cards than others.

2)   The player to the left of the dealer begins by calling on another player and requesting a card, e.g., "Carl, give me an Apollo card."

3)   If the player addressed has the card specified, the card must be given to the first player. As long as the first player is successful in getting cards his or her turn continues. When unsuccessful, the turn passes to the left.

4)   When a player gets all four cards of one god or goddess, the set is shown to all players and placed on the table.

5)   The player collecting the most sets wins.

6)   Note: An alternative game is Monsters or Myth Monsters, played the same as Gods & Goddesses, substituting mythological creatures (*see* illustrations on page 119).

* * *

```
*************************************************************
```
ALLUSIONS
```
*************************************************************
```

PURPOSE: To familiarize students with the Greek mythological origins of some present-day terms.

GRADE LEVEL: 8th grade

TIME: 35 minutes

NUMBER: 4 students per gameboard

METHOD OF CHECKING: Answer sheet

MATERIALS:

1) 1 Allusions gameboard for every 4 players made from 14x22-inch colored posterboard.

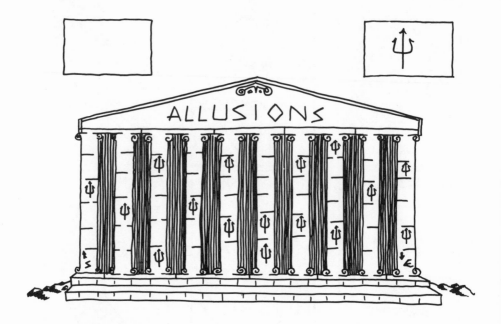

2) 4 markers per gameboard.

3) 1 die per gameboard.

4) 30 3x4-inch colored posterboard cards bearing words from Greek mythology. For example:

Atlas	Amazon
Chimera	Hydra
Gorgons	Sirens
Trojan	Pandora
Muses	Achilles

5) 15 3x4-inch colored posterboard Trident cards bearing directions such as:

Eros (cupid) has pierced your heart—lose one turn
Hermes (Mercury) speeds you on your way—move ahead 4 spaces
Encounter the Chimera—move back 3 spaces
A Trojan comes to your aid—move ahead 2 spaces
Your odyssey begins—move ahead 1 space

6) Answer sheet listing allusions to Greek mythology dry-mounted to a piece of colored posterboard. Examples:

Achilles—a Greek hero whose heel was his weakness. Achilles tendon.

Amazon—women warriors; any woman who is excessively large or strong.

Atlas—a Titan, symbolizing power and strength, who held the heavens on his shoulders. A bone that joins the skull and spine is called Atlas.

Demeter (Ceres)—goddess of grain and growing things. The word cereal comes from Ceres.

Gorgons—monsters who turned all who looked at them into stone. Type of coral called gorgania. Small jellyfish called Medusa.

Hercules—a mortal known for extraordinary size and strength. A herculean task is difficult or impossible.

Hydra—a nine-headed creature that grew two more heads when one was chopped off by Hercules. A hydra-headed evil is something that gets worse as one tries to deal with it.

Muses—nine goddesses who loved song and beautiful things. The words music and museum come from them.

Sirens—loud and beautiful voices drawing sailors' attention. Emergency vehicles use sirens.

Titan—huge gods who controlled the world. Titanic means huge.

Trojan—a person from Troy who fought long and hard. "Works like a Trojan" means determination and hard work.

7) Large manila envelope (16x20-inches) for the materials.

PROCEDURE:

1) Players are given an Allusions gameboard and related materials.

2) Both sets of cards are shuffled and placed face down in the appropriate spaces on the gameboard.

3) Markers are placed on start (S) and players roll the die to determine the order of play.

4) The first player draws a card, reads the word and gives the present day allusion. If correct, the player rolls the die, moves the number of spaces indicated and places the card at the bottom of the pile. If incorrect, no move is made and the next player takes a turn.

5) Correct answers may be verified by the use of the answer sheet. If a dispute arises, the media specialist or teacher acts as arbitrator.

6) When a player lands on a space with a Trident, a Trident card is drawn and directions must be followed.

7) The first player to reach the end (E) is the winner.

* * *

CLICHÉ CHARADES

PURPOSE: To help students become aware of and avoid the use of clichés.

GRADE LEVEL: 7th or 8th grade

TIME: 30 minutes

NUMBER: Small groups (4) to entire class

METHOD OF CHECKING: Self-checking

MATERIALS:
1) 30 3x5-inch index cards bearing clichés such as:

You could have heard a pin drop.
To have a heart of stone
Any port in a storm
Believe it or not
Between the devil and the deep blue sea
The blind leading the blind
Born under a lucky star
Cart before the horse
Rule of thumb
By word of mouth
A chip off the old block
To rain cats and dogs
To sit on the fence
To smell a rat
To cut off one's nose to spite one's face
To face the music
A battle royal
Fate worse than death
Feather in one's cap
To fight tooth and nail
In one's hour of need
Seeing is believing.
In a nutshell
In one ear and out the other
In the same boat
Needle in a haystack
One foot in the grave
Out of the woods
To bury the hatchet

2) A stopwatch or a clock or watch with a second hand.

3) Large manila envelope (10x13-inches) for the materials.

PROCEDURE:
1) The group is divided into two teams and captains are chosen. The captains act as timekeepers.

2) Teams determine order of play and are seated together with one team on one side of the room and the other team on the other side of the room. Cards are placed face down in a pile on a table in front of the teams.

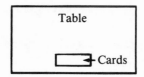

3) The first player draws a card, reads it silently and places it in a discard pile on the table.

4) The player has two minutes to act out the cliché, attempting to get his or her team to guess the cliché within the time allotment (as in Charades).

5) If the team guesses the cliché within two minutes, 5 points are scored. If the cliché is not identified, no points are scored and team 2 takes a turn. If a dispute arises, the media specialist or teacher acts as arbitrator.

6) Teams alternate turns for 30 minutes.

7) The team with the most points wins.

* * *

ALACAZAR

PURPOSE: To help students recognize similes, metaphors, and alliteration.

GRADE LEVEL: 7th or 8th grade

TIME: 30 minutes

NUMBER: 4 students per gameboard

METHOD OF CHECKING: Answer sheet

MATERIALS:
1) 1 Alacazar gameboard for every 4 students playing made from 14x22-inch colored posterboard.

2)   2 dice per gameboard.

3)   4 markers per gameboard.

4)   30 3x4-inch colored posterboard cards bearing sentences with similes, metaphors or alliteration, such as:

People swarmed around the ticket booth like bees around a beehive.
The judge was as silent as the Sphinx.
She wanted to be the largest frog in the pond.
Terrible torrents of rain washed down the gully.
Father said, "You're not reading that blasted book, again!"

5)   15 3x4-inch colored posterboard direction cards bearing directions such as:

Caught by the Wizard's assistant—lose a turn
A fierce dragon is in the chamber—move back 3 chambers to get the magic sword
You have become lost!—Wait 1 turn to get your bearings
The Wizard turns loose his killer bats!—if there are stairs to the next chamber, you
     may escape (1 chamber); if there are no stairs, lose 1 turn

6)   Answer sheet dry-mounted to a piece of colored posterboard.

7)   Large manila envelope (16x20-inches) for the materials.

PROCEDURE:

Form A

1)   Players are given an Alacazar gameboard and related materials.

2)   Cards are placed face down in 2 piles on the table above the gameboard with peril (bat) cards placed next to the question cards.

3)   Markers are placed in the towers on the gameboard and players roll the dice to determine order of play.

4)   The first player draws a question card, reads the sentence aloud and identifies the simile, metaphor, or alliteration in the sentence. Correct answers may be verified by checking the answer sheet.

5)   If correct, the player rolls the dice, moves the number of spaces indicated by the dice and places the card in a discard pile. If incorrect, no move is made, the card is discarded, and the next player takes a turn.

6)   When a player lands on a space marked with a bat, a peril card is drawn and directions must be followed, and the card is placed at the bottom of the pile.

7)   The first player to reach the base of the castle wins.

Form B

Played the same as Form A except players place markers at the base of the castle and move to the towers. The first player to reach the tower wins.

Form C

Played the same as Form A except players place markers at the base of the castle, move to the tower and return to the base again. The first player to return to the base of the castle wins.

* * *

```
*************************************************************
```
MINGLE
```
*************************************************************
```

PURPOSE: To allow students to participate in a creative writing effort.

GRADE LEVEL: 7th or 8th grade

TIME: 45 minutes

NUMBER: 4 students

METHOD OF CHECKING: Student judges

MATERIALS:

1) 2 paper bags, each containing 4 items. The bags need not contain identical items, but may include, for example:

Candle	Compact
Button	Plastic flower

2) Paper and pencils.

PROCEDURE:

1) The students are paired to form two teams and are given the paper bags.

2 Each pair has 20 minutes to create a story involving all four items as integral parts of the story.

3) After 20 minutes, 5 student judges are chosen by the teacher to rate the stories from 1-10 with 10 as high score.

4) Each team reads the story and is rated by the judges and the teacher with the judges giving some reasons for the scores given.

5) The team with the highest score wins.

* * *

```
*************************************************************
```
COMIC CHARACTERS
```
*************************************************************
```

PURPOSE: To allow students to engage in some creative writing resulting in an oral presentation.

GRADE LEVEL: 7th or 8th grade

TIME: Part A — Preparation — 2 class periods of approximately 40 minutes each
Part B — Presentation — 1 class period

NUMBER: 6 students per group

METHOD OF CHECKING: Panel of judges made up of 2 students plus the teacher

MATERIALS:
1) *The World Encyclopedia of Comics* (New York: Chelsea House, c1976), edited by Maurice Horn.

2) Paper and pencils.

3) Mimeographed score sheets for the judges:

SCORE SHEET
Score each group from 1-10 points on creativity, mechanics and presentation.

		Group I	Group II	Group III
CREATIVITY A. Was the presentation well-planned? B. Was it creative?	Score	_____	_____	_____
MECHANICS A. Did the presentors use good grammar? B. Were complex sentences used in the presentation?	Score	_____	_____	_____
PRESENTATION A. Did the presentors know the material? B. Was the presentation done smoothly?	Score	_____	_____	_____

PROCEDURE:
Part A
1) The six players are divided into three groups.

2) Each group consults *The World Encyclopedia of Comics* to choose a character. The teammates determine who is to assume the character's identity and who is to be the reporter and together write a 15-minute interview of the comic character. For example, if the character chosen is Superman some questions might be:

Can you describe the planet of Krypton?
How does it feel to fly as fast as a speeding bullet?
What is your most memorable moment?

(Procedures continue on page 128)

Part B

1) When the teams complete the written interviews, a class period is used for practicing the oral presentations.

2) Before the groups give the presentations, two students are chosen to be judges along with the teacher and are given score sheets and directions for the oral presentation.

3) Team I gives the oral presentation; the judges score the presentation and give results with an explanation of the score. Teams II and III follow the same procedure.

4) The team with the most points wins.

* * *

TERM PAPER TOSSBACK

PURPOSE: To reinforce the procedures to be followed when researching and writing a term paper.

GRADE LEVEL: 7th grade

TIME: 40-50 minutes

NUMBER: Small group

METHOD OF CHECKING: Answer sheet

MATERIALS:

1) The gameboard is the floor of the IMC or classroom covered by squares of colored paper or whatever paper is available; minimum of 50 arranged in whatever order is suitable to physical space.

2) Players are the markers.

3) 2 large wooden blocks made to resemble dice.

4) 36-60 3x5-inch index cards bearing questions on points to remember as the paper is being written. On the front, in the lower right-hand corner, place numbers 2-12 to correspond to dots on the dice; number 2 being the easiest question while number 12 is the hardest question. On the back, place the number 1 through however many cards will be used (1-36) or (1-60); numbers to correspond to those used on answer sheet. Sample questions:

In order to begin research on a term paper, what must first be selected? (a topic)
What key in the library would one use to find sources? (card catalog)
What two parts of a book would be most helpful in selecting appropriate material? (table of contents and index)
Is it necessary to read an entire article or book to obtain information on a topic? (no)
The topic is confirmed, the materials selected — what should be written before taking notes? (an outline)
Notes are traditionally taken on what? (a 3x5-inch index card)
Name four items that should be found on all note cards. (topic, note, author's name and page number from work used)
If a note is taken directly from a source, how do you indicate it is not your wording? (place quotation marks)
Define the word plagiarism. (a failure to acknowledge borrowed material)
When acknowledging a direct quote, what is written at the bottom of the page or on a special page at the end of the term paper? (footnotes)
Name three of the main elements that go into a footnote. (author's name, title, place of publication, copyright date and page number for material used)
Name the three parts of a term paper. (introduction, body, conclusion)
What is a bibliography? (a list of sources used in writing the paper placed in alphabetical order by author's last name on a special page)

5) Index cards bearing numbers 2-12 to indicate the difficulty of question piles.

6) Master list of questions and answers dry-mounted to a piece of colored posterboard. List the question according to the number on the cards (*see* number 4).

7) Small cardboard box for the materials.

PROCEDURE:

1) Before the students arrive, place the squares in a suitable arrangement around the room with a table in the middle.

2) On the table place the answer sheet, dice and index cards arranged in piles 2-12.

3) Appoint a player to hold the answer sheet to determine if the answer given is correct and to assist other players in choosing the appropriate card.

4) Each player rolls one die to determine order of play, with the highest score starting. Other players line up behind, at the starting square, according to numbers rolled.

5) The first player rolls the dice to determine the question to be answered and chooses a card from the appropriate pile.

6) After giving the question number from the back of the card to the student with the answer sheet, the player reads the question and answers it.

7) If correct, the player moves the number of spaces indicated on the dice. If incorrect, he or she does not advance. Cards are placed at the bottom of appropriate piles.

8) If a player lands on a square already occupied, a second question matching the number on the dice is asked of the original occupant. If unable to answer the question correctly, the player who occupied the square first must go back to start. If the original occupant is correct, however, the asking player must go back 5 squares (or to start if on square 1, 2, 3, or 4).

9) Play continues in this fashion with players alternating turns.

10) The first player to reach the finish square wins.

* * *

COMIC COMBAT

PURPOSE: To promote skill in the use of coordinates.

GRADE LEVEL: 7th or 8th grade

TIME: 40 minutes

NUMBER: Form A—16 players; Form B—2 players

METHOD OF CHECKING: Self-checking

MATERIALS:

1) 2 overhead projectors.

2) 2 screens or 2 pieces of white butcher paper taped to a wall.

3) 2 transparencies of a grid.

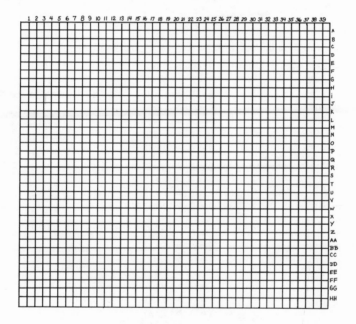

4) 2 sets of 3x4-inch colored posterboard cards bearing instructions for connecting 2 sets of coordinates. The exact number of cards is determined by the size and complexity of each drawing.

(Materials list continues on page 134)

For this picture

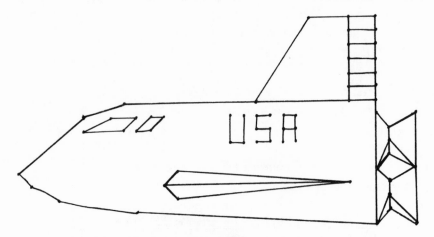

the cards would be labeled with the following instructions:

3•P ► 4•Q		21•K ► 30•K		L•19 ► N•19	
	6•R	28•E ► 28•K		N•19 ► N•20	
	12•S	F•28 ► F•30		N•20 ► L•20	
	30•T	G•28 ► G•30			
	30•E	H•28 ► H•30		L•22 ► L•21	
	25•E	I•28 ► I•30		L•21 ► M•21	
	21•K	J•28 ► J•30		M•21 ► M•22	
	11•K			M•22 ► N•22	
	8•L	L•30 ► M•31		N•22 ► N•21	
	3•P	M•31 ► L•33			
		L•33 ► P•33		N•23 ► L•23	
8•M ► 10•L		P•33 ► N•31		L•23 ► L•24	
10•L ► 12•L		N•31 ► P•30		L•24 ► N•24	
12•L ► 11•M		P•30 ► O•31		M•23 ► M•24	
11•M ► 8•M		O•31 ► P•33			
		O•31 ► M•31			
12•M ► 13•L		P•30 ► Q•31			
13•L ► 14•L		Q•31 ► P•33			
14•L ► 13•M		P•33 ► T•33			
13•M ► 12•M		T•33 ► R•31			
		R•31 ► T•30			
14•Q ► 15•P		T•30 ► S•31			
15•P ► 28•Q		S•31 ► T•33			
28•Q ► 15•R		Q•31 ► S•31			
15•R ► 14•Q					
14•Q ► 28•Q					

5)   2 Vis-A-Vis® pens.

6)   2 tables.

7)   Large manila envelope (12x15-inches) for the materials.

PROCEDURE:

Form A

1)   The tables are arranged with the overhead projectors facing the screens. The cards are shuffled and placed next to the overhead projectors. The transparencies are taped to the projectors and the Vis-A-Vis® pens are placed on the tables.

2) Players are divided into two teams and each team chooses a captain.

3) The captains stand by a table and team members form a line behind each captain, relay fashion.

4) Each captain draws a card, connects the coordinates, places the card in a discard pile, gives the pen to the next player, and goes to the end of the line.

5) Play continues in relay fashion. The winner is the first team to complete the picture.

Form B

Played approximately the same as Form A with one person racing against another person to complete the drawing by using the coordinates given.

* * *

```
*****************************************************************
```
WORLD SAFARI
```
*****************************************************************
```

PURPOSE: To allow students to demonstrate the ability to use an atlas, map, or globe successfully by locating specific places or answering specific questions.

GRADE LEVEL: 7th grade

TIME: 45-50 minutes

NUMBER: Limited to the number of available atlases, maps, or globes

METHOD OF CHECKING: Teacher

MATERIALS:
1) Newspaper clippings of names—cities, provinces, countries. These are best found in the travel section.

2) Two sets of cards (two different colors) 5x7-inches—20 per set.

3) Large manila envelope (12x15-inches) for the materials.

PROCEDURE:
1) Dry mount the newspaper names on the cards, then laminate or cover with clear contact paper.

2) Have the students pretend they are going on a trip to the cities, provinces, or countries named on their cards.

3) Discuss with the students why it is necessary to find out about the places before they visit them—climate factors, customs, culture, and so on.

4) Review or teach latitude and longitude.

5) Review instructions:

   Depending on whether the name on the card is of a city, province, or country, give the following information:
   a) city—what province or country it is located in and its latitude and longitude.
   b) province—what part of the country it is located in and the latitude and longitude of its furthermost extremes.
   c) country—what continent is it located on? If an atlas is used—give the page number the information is found on and the map.

6) On signal, the players locate the necessary atlases, maps, or globes and begin their World Safari in search of the answers.

7) A point is given for each correct answer.

* * *

WORLD COUNTRY-BEE

PURPOSE: To acquaint students with the countries of the world and their capitals.

GRADE LEVEL: 7th grade

TIME: 45-50 minutes

NUMBER: 10 players to an entire class

METHOD OF CHECKING: Answer sheet

MATERIALS:

1) Answer sheets containing the name of the country, its capital, and its general location dry-mounted to a piece of colored posterboard. For example:

Country	Capital	General Location
Australia	Canberra	South Pacific
Bulgaria	Sofia	Balkan Peninsula— Southern Europe
Cambodia	Phnom Penh	Southeast Asia
Dahomey	Porto-Novo	West Africa
Ethiopia	Addis Ababa	Northeast Africa
France	Paris	Western Europe
Greece	Athens	Balkan Peninsula— Southern Europe
Hungary	Budapest	Central Europe
Iceland	Reykjavik	Northern Europe
Jordan	Amman & Jerusalem	Middle East

2) Large manila envelope (12x15-inches) for the materials.

PROCEDURE:

1) Divide the group in half, playing one side against the other.

2) Appoint a scorekeeper to keep the score on the chalkboard.

3) The first player on team 1 gives the name of the country and the opposing player on team 2 gives the capital.

4) If the answer is correct, a point is scored and the player who answered gets to give the next country. If it is incorrect, the play goes to the next player on team 1 who must try to give the correct answer.

5) If both are incorrect, open the question up to volunteers from any team; a player who states the right answer scores two points for his or her team.

6) Play then moves back to the second player on team 2 whose turn was coming up when the volunteer period began.

7) In other words, play moves back and forth from one team to the other.

8) The team with the highest score at the end of the period is the winner.

9) Variation: Instead of naming the capital, have the player approach a world map and point to the country as well as name the general area in which the country is located.

* * *

```
*************************************************************
```
CONGO CRUISE
```
*************************************************************
```

PURPOSE: To promote an interest in and a knowledge of an ever-changing continent.

GRADE LEVEL: 7th grade

TIME: 25-30 minutes

NUMBER: 2-4 players per gameboard

METHOD OF CHECKING: Answer sheet

MATERIALS:
1) 1 gameboard for every four players. The gameboard can be made from 14x22-inch colored posterboard.

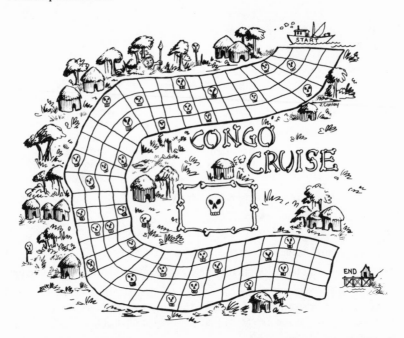

2) 3x4-inch colored posterboard cards with questions or statements, 35 per gameboard. Place a number (1-35) in the lower right-hand corner of each card; this number should correspond to the numbers used on answer sheet. Sample questions and statements:

Name the largest desert in Northern Africa. (Sahara)
What is an oases? (a place in a desert which has enough water to grow crops)
Name the lake from which the White Nile flows. (Lake Victoria)
Name three mountainous countries that have a rainy climate. (Uganda, Kenya, and Tanzania)
What busy city in Egypt was founded by Alexander the Great in 332 B.C.? (Alexandria)
Define the word "nomad." (a person who wanders from place to place without a permanent home)
Which city is known as the "City of Gold"? (Johannesburg)

Name two kinds of freight carried on the Congo River. (up-bound—manufactured goods and petroleum; downsteam—palm oil, rubber, coffee, cotton, peanuts, cacao and rice)

Name the tribe that supplies the most workers for the gold mines. (Bantu)

Name the two capitals of South Africa. (Pretoria and Cape Town)

On the back of each card place a number (1-5) to indicate the number of spaces to be moved during a turn.

3) 15 3x4-inch colored posterboard skull cards bearing specific directions per gameboard. For example:

Unable to find your cache of water-filled eggs in the Kalahari Desert—return to start for new ones

Invited to share in a Berber feast—move ahead two spaces

You are offered the famous drink of the Masai tribe; you refuse—spin the spinner and move double the number fast!

You are caught trying to smuggle diamonds out of the Kimberly mines—lose the next turn

You have produced more than your quota in the gold fields—take another turn

4) 1 master list of questions/statements and answers per gameboard dry-mounted to a piece of colored posterboard. List the questions/statements according to the number on the cards (*see* number 2).

5) 4 markers per gameboard.

6) 1 spinner per gameboard.

7) Large manila envelope (16x20-inches) for the materials.

PROCEDURE:

1) A group of 2-4 players is formed and given a Congo Cruise gameboard and related materials.

2) The Congo Cruise cards and skull cards are placed face down in a pile on the designated areas on the gameboard. All markers are placed at "Start," and each player spins the spinner to determine the order of play.

3) The first player draws a Congo Cruise card and answers the question/statement. The other players may check the answer sheet if in doubt.

4) If correct, the player moves the number of spaces indicated on the back of the card and retains the card. If incorrect, the card is placed at the bottom of the pile and the next player takes a turn.

5) If a player lands on a space with a skull, a skull card is drawn, the directions are followed, and the card is placed at the bottom of the pile.

6) Play continues in this manner with players alternating turns.

7) The first player to reach the finish (or the player who accumulates the most cards) wins.

* * *

****

FEATURES I.D.

****

PURPOSE: To help students recognize the difference between man-made features and natural features.

GRADE LEVEL: 7th or 8th grade

TIME: 30-45 minutes

NUMBER: 2-4 players per gameboard

METHOD OF CHECKING: Self-checking

MATERIALS:

1) 1 14x20-inch white posterboard gameboard for every 4 players.

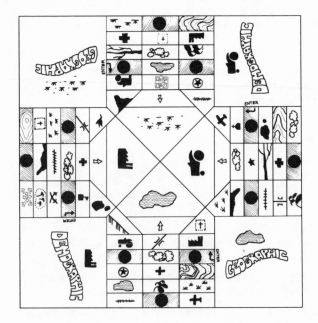

2) Variety of maps—street maps, physical features maps, road maps, political boundary maps, and so on.

3) 2 dice and or 1 spinner for every gameboard.

4) 4 markers per gameboard.

5) Glue.

6) Large manila envelope (16x20-inches) for the materials.

PROCEDURE:

Preparation

Either use the illustration given for a gameboard or vary the symbols by cutting squares from the maps and gluing them in an irregular but fair pattern. Alternate maps showing geographic symbols with maps showing man-made/demographic symbols. For example:

Space 1 – grasslands and marsh
Space 2 – super highways
Space 3 – river and trees
Space 4 – airport area
Space 5 – desert and buildings

Play

1) 2-4 students gather around a designated area and are given the playing materials.

2) Players throw the dice to determine the order of play; the player rolling the highest number begins.

3) If four students play, two students choose to play on man-made (demographic) symbols, and two choose to play on geographic symbols.

4) Players of demographic symbols move only on even numbers and players of physical symbols move only on odd numbers.

5) Each player must keep his or her type of symbol throughout the game. For example, if player 2 decides to play geographic symbols, he or she moves the marker forward from one physical symbol jump to the next (no matter how many spaces are in between), but only when he or she spins or throws an odd number.

6) If a space with a circle is directly in front of the marker the player may move there as a free space.

7) Each player must correctly identify the symbols landed on to earn the right to remain on that space. If an incorrect answer is given, the player must return to the previous resting place.

8) If a player's marker comes to rest on a space occupied by an opponent's marker, the player has captured that marker.

9) When an opponent's marker is captured, it is sent back to its starting space and may be re-entered on the next turn.

10) The only exception is when markers rest on a space with a circle; that is neutral territory.

11) A marker cannot be captured on its HOME BASE since no opponent may enter another player's HOME BASE.

12) An opponent's marker may not be captured on a neutral zone.

13) Play alternates around the group, to the right, until someone returns to his or her home quadrant, climbs the center column, enters the last space, and leaves the board.

14) The winner must throw doubles or spin a predetermined number in order to jump out.

* * *

HISTORICAL HITCHHIKE

PURPOSE: To familiarize students with the history of the area under study.

GRADE LEVEL: 7th or 8th grade

TIME: 30-45 minutes

NUMBER: 3-4 players per gameboard

METHOD OF CHECKING: Self-checking

MATERIALS:

1) 1 gameboard for every 4 players made from 14x22-inch colored posterboard. The gameboard will be a map of the area being studied, marked with historical places. For example: the British Isles

Amesbury—stone monuments (Stonehenge)
Battle—battle scene (Battle of Hasting)
Beaconsfield—towns and inns (robbers den)
Bristol—famous person and/or book (John Cabot sailed from here; Robert L. Stevenson; *Treasure Island*)
Cambridge—university building (college town)
Canterbury—church (famous cathedral)
London—government buildings, tower, museum, palace (House of Parliament; Tower of London; British Museum; Buckingham Palace)
Thames River—boats (Henry VIII's escapades)
Nottingham—castle (Robin Hood)
Oxford—library (Bodleian Library)
Plymouth—ships (Mayflower)
Stratford-upon-Avon—theatre (Shakespeare Theatre)
Tintagel—ruins (King Arthur's castle)
Windsor—document (Runnymede and Magna Carta)
Aberdeen—tolbooth (Old Tolbooth)
Edinburgh—castle (Castle of James I & Holyroodhouse)
Glasgow—factories and foundries (industrial town)
Inverness—monster (Loch Ness Monster)
Perth—palace (Scone Palace)
Cardiff—castle (Cardiff Castle on ruins of Roman fort)
Holyhead—lighthouse and seals (hunting)
Swansea—ships (seaport)
Belfast—castle (Stormont Castle)
Dublin—brewery (Guiness Brewery)
Galway—wall in ruins (Norman Wall)
Killarney—market day (Market town)
Waterford—goblet (Waterford crystal)

2) 3x4-inch colored posterboard cards with questions; 30-50 per gameboard. Number of cards may vary with the area being studied.

A somber collection of large, prehistoric stone monuments.

(Front view)   (Back view)

Sample questions:

Where did King John, under threat of Civil War, affix his seal to the Magna Carta in 1215? (Runnymede)
What famous government building did Guy Fawkes attempt to blow up on November 5, 1605? (House of Parliament)
What country town is famous for the Loch Ness Monster? (Inverness)
What city is the capital and a major manufacturing center of Wales? (Cardiff)
What ancient city was once the home of King Arthur's Castle? (Tintagel)

For best results, each location should have more than one description.

(Materials continue on page 144)

3) 3-4 markers per gameboard.

4) 1 die per gameboard.

5) Large manila envelope (16x20-inches) for the materials.

PROCEDURE:

1) Groups of four are formed by counting off in fours.

2) Each group gathers around a table and is given a gameboard and related materials.

3) The cards are shuffled and placed in a pile where designated on the gameboard. All players place markers in the "start" box.

4) The die is rolled to determine the order of play.

5) The first player draws a card, answers the question/statement, and turns to the verso of the card to check to see if the answer is correct. The answer forms a circle.

6) If correct, the player moves his or her marker to that location and retains the card. If incorrect, the marker either remains at start or at the previous location and the card is returned to the bottom of the pile.

7) Each player may visit a location only once. If a card is drawn for a previous location, it is returned to the bottom of the pile and a turn is "lost."

8) Play continues around the circle, with players alternating turns, until all the cards are gone or time runs out.

9) The player with the most cards at the end is the winner and designated as the best "historian."

* * *

MAPPING THE WAY

PURPOSE: To promote an understanding of the use of road maps.

GRADE LEVEL: 7th or 8th grade

TIME: 5-15 minutes per round

NUMBER: 2-5 players per group

METHOD OF CHECKING: Self-checking

MATERIALS:
1) Road maps of the areas under consideration for mapping—one for each player.
2) 1 stop watch per group.
3) 1 die for each group.
4) Paper and pencils for each group.
5) Large manila envelope (16x20-inches) for the materials.

PROCEDURE:
1) Divide the players into groups of 2-5, hand out the materials, and appoint a scorekeeper for each group.
2) Either cut off the locator guide before handing out the maps or have the students fold it under the rest of the map.
3) Students roll the die to determine the order of play, with the highest score starting.
4) The starting player gives the name of a place found on the map. The scorekeeper sets the stop watch, and times his or her fellow player or players while they attempt to locate the place.
5) Play alternates between players or rotates clockwise around the group if more than two play.
6) The winner at the end of each round of play is the one who locates a place given in the shortest amount of time. A round is complete when each player has had a turn to name a place. If a player locates more than one place, use the lowest recorded time for his or her score.
7) Variations:

   A
   a) Assign the players a trip to take using their maps.
   b) Explain that they may travel between two points of interest, or there may be as many as 20 points through which they must travel.
   c) The winner may be the player who completes his or her journey in the shortest number of miles, or completes the trip first.
   d) A written record may be kept by recording mileage, places seen, and/or highway routes used.

   B
   a) Assign the players a given number of miles to travel and have as an objective the viewing of the greatest number of landmarks, points of interest and towns.
   b) The trip is to be completed within a specific time period.
   c) The winner will be the player who plans ahead and plots the course on the map with a pencil, or by recording mileage and places seen on another sheet of paper.

* * *

****

RACE THE MOUNTAIN

****

PURPOSE: To familiarize students with general knowledge about the countries under consideration.

GRADE LEVEL: 7th or 8th grade

TIME: 25-30 minutes per round

NUMBER: 3-5 players per gameboard

METHOD OF CHECKING: Answer sheet

MATERIALS:

1) 1 gameboard for every five players made from 14x22-inch colored posterboard.

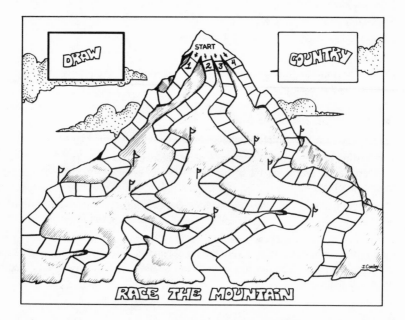

2) 3x4-inch colored posterboard cards with questions or statements; 30-50 per gameboard. The questions or statements should be general enough that they fit any country under consideration. Place a number in the lower right-hand corner of each card; this number should correspond to those used on the answer sheet. Sample questions or statements:

What city is the capital of your country?
Name two main occupations of the people from your country.
What type of government leads your nation?
What type of climate does your country have?
Name one mountain range located in your country.

3) 8 3x4-inch colored posterboard cards per gameboard bearing the name of a country. For example: France, Spain, Sweden, Norway, Finland, Germany, Austria, and Switzerland.

4)   8 3x4-inch colored posterboard direction cards per gameboard. For example:

Wax correct for snow conditions — go ahead three spaces
Icy course — lose control, go off course — start over
Catch tip on gate — lose next turn
Tip breaks — go back to start
Perfect snow conditions — go ahead two spaces
White-out condition — go back three spaces
Hit mogul going too fast, sent airborne ahead two spaces
Binding releases unexpectedly — lose next turn

5)   1 master list of questions/statements and answers per gameboard, dry-mounted to a piece of colored posterboard. List the questions/statements according to the number on the cards (*see* materials 2).

6)   4 markers per gameboard.

7)   1 die per gameboard.

8)   Large manila envelope (16x20-inches) for the materials.

PROCEDURE:

1)   Players form groups of 3-5, and are given a Race the Mountain gameboard and related materials.

2)   Students roll the die to determine the order of play, with the lowest score starting on trail #1.

3)   One player is elected to hold the answer sheet in each round, thereby becoming the judge, and determines whether a given answer is correct. This student does not participate in the round but indicates whether a player has answered correctly and may therefore move. The judge also settles disputes should they arise.

4)   Players place markers at the start position on appropriate trails and the shuffle question/statement cards with the direction cards, placing them face down on "draw card" box.

5)   Place the country cards face down on the "country" box.

6)   Each contestant draws a card from the "country" box to determine what country he or she represents in the race.

7)   Contestant number 1 draws a card, gives the number located in the lower right-hand corner, and answers the question/statement.

8)   The judge indicates whether the answer is correct or incorrect. If correct, the contestant moves the marker one space and retains the card. If incorrect, the marker is not moved, the card is returned to the bottom of the pile, and the next player takes a turn.

9)   Play continues with contestants alternating turns.

10) Some cards are included that do not require an answer; but require the contestant to start over, to move ahead, to go back or to lose next turn. If a contestant draws one of these cards the directions must be followed. When the direction has been followed, the card is placed at the bottom of the "draw" pile.

11) The contestant with the most cards, at the end, is the winner.

* * *

TOP OF THE NEWS

PURPOSE: To acquaint students with current events and famous people in the news.

GRADE LEVEL: 7th and 8th grade

TIME: 10-15 minutes per round

NUMBER: Small group to an entire class

METHOD OF CHECKING: Teacher

MATERIALS:
1) Chalkboard, chalk, and eraser. An example of categories for the Top of the News board:

Political Campaigns	Olympics	Mideast
Potpourri	State News	World News
World Leaders in the News	Famous People in the News	Sports

2) Master list of categories and questions like those below dry-mounted to a piece of colored posterboard.

   1. Name the Republican candidate and the Democratic candidate for president in the 1980 election. (Ronald Reagan and Jimmy Carter)
   2. Which male won the most medals for speed skating in the 1980 Winter Olympics? (Eric Heiden)
   3. When did the "oil" or "religious" war between Iraq and Iran break out? (September 1980)
   4. Name the congressman in the House of Representatives who was expelled for accepting a bribe in the FBI's Abscam undercover operation; the first since the outbreak of the Civil War. (Michael Myers)
   5. Name the current governor of your state.
   6. What nation helped six Americans excape from Iran during the hostage period? (Canada)

7. What is the name of the first female prime minister in British history? (Margaret Thatcher)
8. Name the candidate in the 1980 election who ran on the independent ticket. (John Anderson)
9. Who was the flamboyant coach of the Colorado Rockies for the 1979-80 season? (Don Cherry)

3) A coin of any denomination.

4) Large manila envelope (12x15-inches) for the materials.

PROCEDURE:

1) Divide the students into two evenly matched teams; choose team captains.

2) The captain becomes team spokesman and makes all the decisions for the team.

3) The team captain whose last name is closest to the beginning of the alphabet is first to call "heads" or "tails" and flips the coin. Whichever leader calls the flip correctly begins.

4) The captain consults the team and selects a category from the Top of the News board.

5) The teacher or an appointed student asks team 1 a question about the category selected.

6) The captain may answer or choose a teammate to answer the question (preferably one who has volunteered).

7) Once the captain has selected the person to answer, no one else may assist in answering.

8) The first answer is accepted. If the answer is correct, an "X" or "O" is placed in the space. If the student answers incorrectly, team 2 has the opportunity to answer the question.

9) If team 2 accepts the challenge and answers the question correctly, they get that square and may select another category for a possible two in a row. If, however, they answer incorrectly they do not receive a second category and the turn goes back to team 1.

10) No team may earn an "X" or "O" without answering a qeustion correctly.

11) If team 2 decides, however, not to answer the other team's missed question, they select their own category but do not receive a second turn.

12) The first team to score three "X"s or three "O"s in a row horizontally, vertically or diagonally wins the game.

13) In the event that no team scores in the manner stated above, the team with the most "X"s or "O"s wins the game.

* * *

****
BIOGRAPHIES
****

PURPOSE: To promote an interest in famous or well-known persons throughout history.

GRADE LEVEL: 7th or 8th grade

TIME: 50 minutes

NUMBER: 2-6 players per gameboard

METHOD OF CHECKING: Self-checking

MATERIALS:

1) 3x4-inch colored posterboard cards depicting the various categories of information that would provide a "silhouette" biography. For example:

   yellow—place (country or continent)
   blue—time (century)
   green—letter (A-Z and 10 wild cards)
   orange—activity (government, military, head of state, clergy, and so on)
   red—status (dead or alive, male or female, real or folkhero)

The number of cards will depend upon the amount of cards needed for each category to complete the intended biographical "silhouette."

2) 22x28-inch white posterboard for the gameboard.

3) 1 die per gameboard.

4) Availability of dictionaries, encyclopedias, almanacs, and so on.

5) Paper for score sheets and pencils.

6) Large manila envelope (12x15-inches) for the materials; excluding the gameboard.

PROCEDURE:

1) 2-6 players gather around a designated area and are given the appropriate materials.

2) Appoint a player as dealer. The dealer combines all cards (letter and "silhouette") and shuffles thoroughly. Six cards are dealt face down to each player, while ten cards are dealt face up on the board in the matching color area (place card on place star, letter card on letter star, and so on) — these cards will be referred to as "board cards." The remainder of the deck is placed face down in the area marked "silhouette."

3) Choose one player to keep score.

4) The students roll the die to determine the order of play, with the highest score starting.

5) A player may do one or more of the following during a turn:

Begin a biography: start the biography on any of the four sides by placing the first card in the space with the star and succeeding cards on the next open spaces. Letter cards must be reserved for completing the biography. A player may start more than one biography.

Continue an existing biography: add cards to any biography on the board.

Change an existing biography: place a card over one already played to the biography to change it. The new card, however, must match the category already placed (letter to letter, time to time, and so on). As a result, a biography may be changed to benefit the existing player or prevent another player from completing the portrait, but the player must be able to defend the change if challenged by identifying the person the changed biography applies to (*see* procedure 9).

Complete the biography: end a biography of 4 or more cards by playing a letter card, either from the board or hand, which corresponds to the first letter of the person's last name. It is possible to end more than one biography during a turn.

Play to no existing biography: place up to 4 cards in hand on their matching board area and draw new cards from the deck to replace them.

6) A player completes his or her turn by calling out the name of the person who fits the constructed "silhouette," picking up all the cards in that biography, and having the scorekeeper record the score (number of points in space in which the letter card was played). More points can be scored by finishing a biography with more than one initial (letter) card (in sequence) and by playing additional status cards to further identify the "biographee."

7) Stack completed biographies to the players left with the letter card on top so that other players may see what letters have been played.

8) The player replenishes his or her hand by drawing cards from the deck and dealing cards to the board to replace those used. Place each board card in its correct area.

9) A challenge may be made in the following manner at the completion of a turn: if the biography was not finished, a player must name the personage in mind. When a challenge occurs, the other players may refer to the available reference materials (dictionary, encyclopedia, almanac, and so on).

10) If the player was bluffing, he or she must retrieve all cards played in the last turn off the challenged biography and return them to the bottom of the "silhouette" deck, and take a deduction of ten points from final score.

11) If the player was correct, he or she picks up all cards in the biography and scores the full ten points regardless of the number of cards in the "silhouette."

12) Play continues around the board, in a clockwise direction, with players alternating turns until either the deck is exhausted or one player has used up all the cards in his or her hand.

13) The scorekeeper totals the scores and deducts two points for each "silhouette" card and three points for each "letter" card remaining in a player's hand.

14) The player with the highest score wins.

* * *

LAND HO!

PURPOSE: To acquaint students with men who explored unknown lands and crossed uncharted seas.

GRADE LEVEL: 8th grade

TIME: 40 minutes

NUMBER: Small group to an entire class

METHOD OF CHECKING: Teacher and/or answer sheet

MATERIALS:
1) The reference section of an IMC or library.

2) 10-50 4x6-inch oak-tag question cards bearing the name of the explorer, his nationality, noted accomplishments, and a bonus question. For example:

PEDRO ALVARES CABRAL
nationality?
noted for?
bonus question: Where was Cabral headed when he made his discovery?

SIR FRANCES DRAKE
nationality?
noted for?
bonus questions: 1. What was the cruel fate of Drake on his last voyage?
2. What country was most angered by Drake's voyages and why?
3. What famous queen sent him on his voyages?

SAMUEL de CHAMPLAIN
nationality?
noted for?
bonus questions: 1. What city did he establish in the New World?
2. What Indian tribe did he befriend thus ensuring the wrath of another?

3) Answer sheets dry-mounted to pieces of colored posterboard.

4) Large manila envelope (12x15-inches) for the materials.

PROCEDURE:
1) Place the question cards face down on a table.

2) Two teams are formed by counting off in twos, but each student plays as an individual.

3) Team 1 or team 2 draws cards first (order to be determined by teacher) and proceeds to the reference section to track down the answers. The other team follows the same procedure.

4) The players choose a reference work and fill in all the missing information from the printed card on a separate piece of paper.

5) When questions are answered, players exchange sheets with the opposing team and compare the answers with those on the answer sheet. Or, they choose a new card from those face down on the table and begin again, while the teacher corrects the sheet(s).

(Procedures continue on page 154)

6) Scoring:
   a. A player receives one point for each correct answer and loses one point for each incorrect answer.
   b. If the bonus question is correct, one-three points are scored depending on the number of parts. Players do not lose any points if they are unable to answer the bonus question(s).

7) If a player's score is ten or over, he or she is doing quite well; if it is below ten and above zero, more knowledge of explorers is needed; if he or she drops below zero, more time should be spent on research.

8) Those players who go right to the top and score 20 or more can start looking around for ships of their own. Bon voyage!

9) The team with the most points is declared the winner.

* * *

EXPLORING EARTH

PURPOSE: To expand knowledge of land and ocean as they exist today.

GRADE LEVEL: 8th grade

TIME: Part I—2 class periods; Part II—2 class periods

NUMBER: Small group to an entire class

METHOD OF CHECKING: Teacher and student judges

MATERIALS:

1) Examples of early world maps, explorers' reports or journals, and modern maps.

2) A list of explorers and adventurers. For example:

Meriwether Lewis	James Cook
William Clark	Henry the Navigator
Henry Hudson	Leif Eriksson
Sir Walter Raleigh	Marco Polo
Christopher Columbus	Sir Francis Drake
Vitus Bering	Roald Amundsen
Oliver Perry	Thor Heyerdahl
Ferdinand Magellan	Vasco Núñez de Balboa

3) Modeling clay and/or map flags.

4) Almanacs, historical atlases, encyclopedias, biographies, and so on.

5) 3x5-inch index cards bearing questions such as:

What kinds of data did the explorer or adventurer add to the map?
What kind of data was he looking for?
What did he know about the region he was exploring?
What surprised him about the unexplored territory?
What special tool did he use in exploration? (e.g., compass, sextant, camera)
How did the region's position on earth affect the expedition?
Why hadn't the region been mapped earlier?
Was any special report made of the expedition?
How has the region changed?

6) 1 timer.

7) Large manila envelope (12x15-inches or 16x20-inches) for the materials.

PROCEDURE:

Part I

1) Divide the participants into groups of two to work together on researching a chosen individual.

2) Explain that they are to undertake a search to unearth information about their explorer's voyage and/or discovery. Take notes on the route used, important features, why the data gained became useful, key landmarks, and so on.

3) When the research is completed, give the students modern maps, modeling clay, and/or map flags. Have them plot on a map some of the main features along the route of the trip and compare them to the region as it exists today.

4) Oral presentations may be made to the class in order to share the information.

(Procedures continue on page 156)

Part II

1) Divide half of the participants into two evenly matched teams and choose a leader for each. The remaining students act as judges.

2) Each team sits in a semicircle on the floor or in chairs with the leader in the middle.

3) Determine the order of the teams.

4) The teacher asks any question related to the material being studied of the first team and sets the timer for one minute.

5) Team members are to confer with each other and the leader is to pick someone to answer before the timer rings.

6) The player chosen to answer must identify his or her explorer or adventurer, then answer the question.

7) Student judges respond with a thumb-up if the answer is correct or with a thumb-down if the answer is incorrect. The teacher is the final authority if the student judges are undecided or incorrect in their judgment.

8) If the answer is correct, the team receives two points; if not, the opposing team has a chance to answer correctly and then take an additional turn.

9) The leaders are to alternate their choices of players to answer so that everyone has a chance.

10) The team with the most points wins.

11) Game may be played one or more times, depending upon class interest and desire to share information.

* * *

****
EXPLORATION CRISS-CROSS
****

PURPOSE: To recall the colorful characters from the American past who explored the continent and to give a point of identification for each of these men.

GRADE LEVEL: 8th grade

TIME: 40-50 minutes

NUMBER: The availability of encyclopedias

METHOD OF CHECKING: Teacher or game leader via answer sheet

MATERIALS:

1) Various sets of encyclopedias.

2) 50 3x4-inch colored posterboard cards, each with different encyclopedia questions printed on them. For example:

   This man claimed the California area for the Spanish. (Cabrillo)
   This Englishman attempted a colony on Newfoundland, and has a famous half-brother named Sir Walter Raleigh. (Humphrey Gilbert)
   A famous attempt at colonization by the English, this colony disappeared without a trace. (Roanoke)
   This Spanish queen is said to have sold her jewels to help Columbus. (Queen Isabella)
   This settler is famous for being saved by an Indian princess. (John Smith)
   This man is given credit for going around the world first, even though he was killed in the Philippines. (Ferdinand Magellan)
   Spanish explorer who traveled into the interior of the United States hunting for the Seven Cities of Gold. (Francisco Coronado)
   This French explorer attempted to find the mouth of the Mississippi River, failed, and was murdered by his men. (Sieur de La Salle)
   French city in Canada that started as a fur-trading post. (Quebec)
   The division between Spain and Portugal that divided the world was called the _____ of Demarcation. (Line)

3) On the verso of each card, place the number, 1-50, to correspond to the answers on the answer sheet.

4) Answer sheet dry-mounted to a piece of colored posterboard.

5) Large manila envelope (12x15-inches) for the materials.

PROCEDURE:

1) Teacher to appoint a game leader, if one is desired, to check answers.

2) Divide the students into two evenly matched teams.

3) Place the question cards face down on a table.

4) Each player chooses a card with a question that can be answered by looking in an encyclopedia.

5) When the information is located, the player either writes the answer on a sheet of paper or shows the teacher or game leader the correct answer and chooses a second card.

6) When eight cards have been successfully answered, a player may help someone else on the team.

7) The first team to answer all of their questions correctly wins the game.

8) For each correct answer, the player also scores one point.

* * *

```
**********************************************************
```
PLAN A CITY!
```
**********************************************************
```

PURPOSE: To demonstrate the complexities involved in starting a new civilization in a strange country.

GRADE LEVEL: 8th grade

TIME: 5 class periods

NUMBER: 6 students per group

METHOD OF CHECKING: Student judges and teacher

MATERIALS:

1) Building materials—toothpicks, ice cream stick, glue, scissors, staples, wire, craft knife, paints, brushes, clay, plaster, flour, colored paper and posterboard, stones, and so on.

2) Reference materials in the media center or any source that will give the required material.

3) Mimeograph Plan A City sheets:

  I.   Describe location
       1. Topography and all surface features of land
       2. Geology
  II. Describe job opportunities
       1. Primary
       2. Secondary
       3. Tertiary
  III. Keep one page of records of:
       1. Laws
          a. criminal
          b. civil
       2. Religious
       3. History
       4. Ethnic grouping
       5. Job opportunities
       6. Literary work the city has produced
       7. The arts
          a. architecture
          b. drama
          c. painting
          d. music
       8. Government
  IV. Types of cities—how they are primarily oriented
       1. Industrial
       2. Financial
       3. Cultural
       4. Resort
       5. Educational
       6. Military
       7. Government
       8. Potpourri—combine any two or three
  V.   Build a scale model of the city you have created
  VI. Research a city of the past—write a newspaper article about the city. Use a headline and a by-line—make the story interesting. You lived at that time so write in the present tense—all members of the group are required to do this one.

4) Mimeographed score sheets for judges:

SCORE SHEET

Score each group from 1-10 points on creativity, mechanics, and presentation.

		Group I	Group II	etc.
CREATIVITY	Score	_____	_____	
A. Was the presentation well planned?				
B. Were the visuals well done?				
C. Was the city accurate to scale?				
MECHANICS	Score	_____	_____	
A. Was there evidence of solid research?				
B. Did the presentors use good grammar?				
C. Were complex sentences and thoughts used in the presentation?				
PRESENTATION	Score	_____	_____	
A. Did the presentors know the material?				
B. Was the presentation done smoothly?				
C. Was the eye contact with the audience adequate?				

---

5) Paper, pencils, and pens.

PROCEDURE:

Part A

1) Divide the class into groups of six students each and hand out the sheet explaining the city plan (*see* materials 3).

2) Go over the plan answering any questions the future planners may have.

3) Groups should use the media center for research and the classroom for building.

4) When a group completes the research and building, a class period should be used to put together and practice the oral presentation.

Part B

1) Before the groups give the presentation, give the student judges (the class members not presenting) the score sheets and directions for the oral presentation.

2) Group leaders choose a number from a box.

3) Group I gives the oral presentation, judges (students and teacher) score the presentation and give the results with an explanation of the score. The other groups follow the same procedure.

4) The group with the highest score wins.

* * *

CRYPTIC SCAVENGER HUNT

PURPOSE: To develop skill in locating information about famous people or events during the Revolution and the Republic era of American history.

GRADE LEVEL: 8th grade

TIME: 40-60 minutes

NUMBER: The availability of reference material

METHOD OF CHECKING: Teacher and/or answer sheet

MATERIALS:

1) The reference section of an IMC or library.

2) 4x4-inch colored posterboard clue cards. Only statements should be typed or lettered on the cards. The number of cards will depend upon the final word or message to be decoded. For example:

    If the Declaration of Independence was written by John Adams, place an *E* in the second space. If he did not write that document, place an *O* there.

    In the first space write an *I* if George Washington won the Battle of Trenton; an *R* if he lost.

    Place a *V* in the third space if the Marquis de Lafayette was appointed inspector general of the Revolutionary forces in 1777, a *T* if he was not.

    Write an *L* in space seven if Francis Marion was the "Swamp Fox"; a *T* if he was not.

    Place an *E* in the sixth space if the colonial troops fought the British at Brandywine Creek; if not, write a *U* instead.

    In the fourth space place a *V* if Benedict Arnold was once a popular colonial general; otherwise, write an *O* in this space.

    If the Battle of Saratoga is known as "the turning point" place an *N* in the ninth space; if not, write an *O* instead.

    Place a U in the fifth space if the artillery and engineering skills of Thaddeus Kosciusko helped secure the victory at Saratoga; if not, write an *L* instead.

    Write an *R* in space eight if the Rhode Island First Regiment was composed of black slaves and free men who withstood a four hour assault during the Battle of Rhode Island in 1778. Place an *I* if it was not.

    If the signers of the Declaration were Royalists, place an *N* in the tenth space. If the Tories were Loyalists, write an *O* in that space.

    Now unscramble the letters to discover the war in which these men were involved or the events occurred.

I	O	T	V	U	E	L	R	N	O	=
1	2	3	4	5	6	7	8	9	10	

REVOLUTION

or

If the Battle of New Orleans occurred during the War of 1812, write an *I* in space nine. If it came after the war was over, place an *I* in space ten.

Place an *N* above number twelve if New England wanted peace and commerce. If it wanted war, place an *N* in the second space.

If the Americans successfully invaded Canada in 1812, write a *C* in the first space. If they were not successful in their 1812 invasion attempts, place a *C* above number nine.

Place a *T* above number nine if the Battle of Tippecanoe was fought in 1811. Place the *T* in the fourth space if it occurred during the war.

If James Madison was president during the War of 1812, place a *U* above number eight. If James Monroe was president at this time, write a *U* in space five.

If Oliver Hazard Perry earned his fame as a noteworthy general during the War of 1812, place an *O* in space eight. If he was known as a famous naval officer, place an *O* in the eleventh space.

If the death of Chief Tecumseh signaled the end of effective Indian assistance to the British, write an *S* in the fourth space. If it did not, place the *S* in the second space.

If the Treaty of Ghent ended the War of 1812, write an *O* in the second space. If the Treaty of Paris ended the war, place an *O* in the first space.

If "America" was written as the result of a bombardment during the War of 1812, write a *T* in space ten. If "The Star-Spangled Banner" was written for that reason, place a *T* in the seventh place.

Place a *T* in the fifth space if "Old Ironsides" was the nickname for the "Constitution." If it was the nickname for the United States, place the *T* in space six.

If "Stonewall" Jackson fought the British during the War of 1812, write an *N* in the fourth space. If "Old Hickory" Jackson fought at New Orleans, write the *N* in the third space.

Place an *I* in the sixth space if the impressment of American sailors by England contributed to the war. If it was not a factor, place an *I* in the seventh space.

Now name the greatest warship of 1812.

C	O	N	S	T	I	T	U	T	I	O	N
1	2	3	4	5	6	7	8	9	10	11	12

3) Master list of clues and answers dry-mounted on a piece of colored posterboard for the use of the teacher and/or students.

4) Paper and pencils.

5) Large manila envelope (12x15-inches) for the materials.

PROCEDURE:

1) Divide the students into two evenly matched teams.

2) Place the clue cards for each team on a table around which team members have gathered.

3) The teacher reminds the players that any reference materials may be used.

4) Each team member chooses a card and searches out the answer. If any cards remain on the table, the players who finish first should choose second cards and search again.

5) When all cards have been chosen and the answers located, team members gather back at the table and pool their answers.

6) Depending upon the form used, the clue has to be unscrambled or can be spelled out clearly. For example, in the first set of clues, the answer spells out *IOTVUELRNO* which must be unscrambled to spell out the war in which the men were involved or the events occurred: *REVOLUTION*. In the second set of clues, the answer spells out *CONSTITUTION* which was the name of one of the great warships of the War of 1812.

7) The team to find all the clues correctly and to answer the final question is declared the winner.

* * *

```
*************************************************************
```
SECTIONALISM SCRAMBLE
```
*************************************************************
```

PURPOSE: To acquaint students with sectionalism — its background, personalities, and conflicts.

GRADE LEVEL: 8th grade

TIME: 40-50 minutes

NUMBER: 2-4 players per gameboard

METHOD OF CHECKING: Answer sheet

MATERIALS:

1) 1 Sectionalism Scramble gameboard made from 14x22-inch colored posterboard for every 4 players.

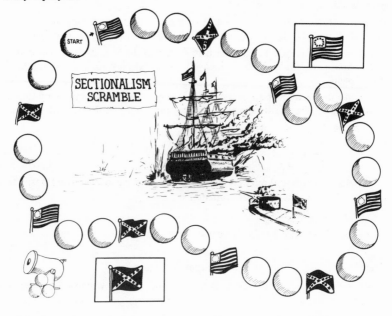

2) Appropriate reference books such as: *Collier's* or *Encyclopedia Americana, The Times Atlas of World History*, and *An Encyclopedic Dictionary of American History*.

3) 4 markers per gameboard.

4) 1 die per gameboard.

5) 1 master list of questions and sources per gameboard, dry-mounted to a piece of colored posterboard. List the questions according to the number on the cards (*See* materials 6).

6) 3x4-inch colored posterboard cards with questions, 30 per gameboard. Do not indicate the reference book to be used to answer the questions. Instead, place a number (1-30) in the lower right-hand corner of each card; the number should

correspond to those used on the answer sheet. The following are the types of questions appropriate to each type of reference work:

Encyclopedia

What was the effect of the dispute over slavery on the admission of Texas to the Union?

What major industrial innovations took place in the 1850s?

What were the causes and effects of the Panic of 1857?

What were some evidences of the Manifest Destiny spirit before 1845?

How and why did President Jackson introduce the spoils system into the federal government?

What was the importance of the Supreme Court's decision in the Dred Scott case?

What was President Buchanan's attitude toward secession?

How did the Battle of Gettysburg signal the turning point of the Civil War?

How did the Civil War affect civilians in the South? In the North?

What changes took place in the Midwest during the war years? How did Congress attempt to aid agriculture?

Historical atlas

What were three different routes used by California-bound gold seekers?

Approximately how much territory was added to our country by acquisitions from Spain and France in the early nineteenth century?

Why did Union generals believe Richmond to be a key position?

What naval actions took place during the first two years of the war?

Why was it important that the Confederacy maintain control of the Mississippi River?

Name the different frontiers in American history and the routes used by each.

What states were leading in cotton growing in 1840?

How many men were enlisted in the Confederate Army as opposed to the Union Army?

By 1865, how many Union ships patrolled the southern coast in a blockade effort?

Historical dictionary

What does the phrase "Manifest Destiny" mean? How did it come into use?

What is an "abolitionist"? Define without using the word abolition.

Define the "spoils system."

What is meant by "popular sovereignty"?

What was the Wilmot Proviso?

Define "King Cotton."

What were the Jim Crow laws?

Where did John Brown's raid take place?

What were the Force Acts in relation to the Reconstruction era?

Who was the Republican party's first candidate?

For best results, use a different set of questions for each gameboard.

7) 3 3x4-inch colored posterboard cards that bear a small picture of a Confederate flag and three that bear a Union flag per gameboard.

8) Large manila envelope (16x20-inches) for the materials.

PROCEDURE:

1) The students are divided into groups of four, and each group is given a gameboard and related materials.

2) The students roll the die to determine the order of play; with the student rolling highest number starting.

(Procedures continue on page 164)

3) Question cards and "flag cards" are shuffled together and placed face down on the "Sectionalism Scramble" gameboard; one-half on the Confederate flag and one-half on the Union flag.

4) All players place markers at "start."

5) The starting student rolls the die, and draws a card from the pile.

6) The player tells in which reference book to look for the answer. If correct, the player moves the number of spaces indicated on the die, and places the card at the bottom of the pile.

7) If incorrect, the player does not move and the card is placed at the bottom of the pile. The other players may use the answer sheet to determine whether a player answers correctly.

8) All other players take turns, following the same procedure.

9) When a "flag card" is drawn, the player calls out "Scramble," and all markers ahead of the marker of the student drawing the card must return to start.

10) If a player lands on a flag, an extra turn may be taken.

11) The first player to reach "start" after circling the board is the winner.

* * *

WILD AND WOOLLY WEST

PURPOSE: To familiarize students with the complexity and variety of frontier life as it yielded to conditions and pressures.

GRADE LEVEL: 8th grade

TIME: 40-50 minutes

NUMBER: 2-6 players per gameboard

METHOD OF CHECKING: Answer sheet

MATERIALS:
1) 1 Wild and Woolly West gameboard made from 14x22-inch colored posterboard for every 6 players.

2) 3x4-inch colored posterboard cards with questions, 35 per gameboard. Place a number (1-35) in the lower right-hand corner of each card; the numbers should correspond to those used on the answer sheet. For best results, each set of questions should be based on different facets of frontier life. Sample questions:

What man was a United States marshal in Tombstone in the 1880s and took part in the O.K. Corral shooting in 1881? (Wyatt Earp)

This man was known as a buffalo hunter and plainsman who in later life organized a Wild West Show. (Wild Bill Hickok)

This woman was the leader of a gang of horse thieves. (Belle Starr)

Which female was known for her horsemanship, marksmanship, and hard drinking? On several expeditions into wild territory she disguised herself as a man. (Calamity Jane)

(Materials list continues on page 166)

This daring man was, at one time, a United States marshal who met his death when he and his gang attempted to rob the Coffeyville, Kansas bank. (Bob Dalton)

3) 6 3x4-inch direction cards per gameboard. Tailor the directions to fit the other cards. For example:

You lose your way exploring a bank vault — lost next two turns trying to find the exit.

You stumble onto the hideout of Jesse James — advance four spaces quickly!

You escape from the clutches of the Dalton Gang — go back five spaces to ensure loss of tracks.

You are a key witness to the murders at the O.K. Corral — advance or go back to the Badlands.

You are caught red-handed stealing horses — go back to "Start."

You are being tried in Judge Isaac Parker's Hanging Court — escape and advance three spaces.

4) 1 master list of questions and answers per gameboard, dry-mounted to a piece of colored posterboard. List the questions according to the number on the cards (*See* materials 2).

5) 6 markers per gameboard.

6) 1 die per gameboard.

7) Large manila envelope (16x20-inches) for the materials.

PROCEDURE:

1) Players form groups of six and are given a Wild and Woolly West gameboard and related materials.

2) Players place markers at "Start" and shuffle all cards, placing them face down near the gameboard.

3) Students roll the die to determine the order of play; the player with the highest score begins.

4) The starting player rolls the die, draws a card, and answers the question.

6) If correct, the player moves the marker the number of spaces indicated by the die and places the card in a discard pile. If incorrect, the player does not move the marker, the card is returned to the bottom of the pile, and the next player takes a turn.

7) Some cards are included that do not require an answer, but require the player to lose a turn, to move ahead, to go back, or to return to start. If a player draws one of these cards, the directions must be followed.

8) Play continues with players alternating turns.

9) The first player to reach "End" is the winner.

* * *

```
******************************************************************
```
THE ROARING TWENTIES: AND A BIT BEFORE AND AFTER
```
******************************************************************
```

PURPOSE: To give students a close look at events and people of those wild and exciting days.

GRADE LEVEL: 8th grade

TIME: 15 minutes per card

NUMBER: The number of available reference materials

METHOD OF CHECKING: Answer sheet and/or teacher

MATERIALS:
1) The reference section of an IMC or library.

2) 6x9-inch oak-tag sheets bearing events to be placed in proper chronological order. For example:

Political events in high circles:	
Assassination of President McKinley	(1901)
Ballinger-Pinchot Controversy	(1910)
President Harding dies in office	(1923)
Passage of the 16th Amendment	(1913)
Establishment of the Tennessee Valley Authority	(1933)
Formation of the League of Nations	(1919)

or

Thought and culture:	
Inauguration of the Pulitzer Prize Awards	(1917)
Enactment of an international copyright law	(1891)
Formation of the first Civic Theater	(1919)
Origination of the Ziegfeld Follies	(1907)
Establishment of the nickelodeon	(1905)
Pan-American Exposition	(1901)

For best results, each card should bear a different category of events.

3) Answer sheet with the events in correct chronological order and the date for each event within a category dry-mounted to a piece of colored posterboard—for use by the students or teacher.

4) 1 timer.

5) Pens and paper.

6) Large manila envelope (12x15-inches) for the materials.

PROCEDURE:
1) Divide the participants into two evenly matched teams. Appoint a team captain.

2) Place the oak-tag cards with the scrambled events on a table.

3) Have the players choose a card.

4) Explain to them that this is a "scavenger hunt." They are first to look up the events and record the dates, and second to place the events in proper sequential order on a separate piece of paper. This is to be done within a 15-minute time span for each card using whatever reference books are available.

(Procedures continue on page 168)

5)   Set the timer for 15 minutes.

6)   At the end of 15 minutes cards are returned to the table, new ones chosen, and the "hunt" resumes.

7)   Play can either end after two rounds or continue for a third round, depending on time, material to be covered, or practice needed in using varied reference works.

8)   The prepared answer sheets can be used in one of two ways: students from team 1 may check the answers of team 2 members and vice versa, or answers may be checked by the teacher and reported to the players.

9)   Both accuracy and speed count toward overall team points. For each item correctly answered (dates and chronological order), one point is scored. For the example "Political events in high circles," given in the materials section, the player and team would score 12 points if everything were answered correctly.

10)   The team with the most accumulated points wins the scavenger hunt.

* * *

WORLD WARS DICTIONARY

PURPOSE: To acquaint students with terms and nicknames used in World Wars I and II.

GRADE LEVEL: 8th grade

TIME: 45-50 minutes

NUMBER: Determined by the availability of reference materials

METHOD OF CHECKING: Answer sheet and/or teacher

MATERIALS:

1) 50 3x3-inch colored posterboard cards with terms or nicknames used in World Wars I and II. For example:

Triple Entente	V-J Day
Battlewagon	Kamikaze
Quisling	Lusitania
Zimmerman note	Flat top
Blitzkrieg	Mulberry
Blood and Guts	Sitzkrieg
Monty	Il Duce
Schlieffen Plan	Ike
Wolf Pack	Desert Fox
Hedgehog	Buzz bumb

Number the cards (1-50) in the lower right-hand corner.

2) Dictionaries, encyclopedias or text books.

3) Answer sheet with the terms and meanings to correspond with numbered cards. For example:

Triple Entente — a power block consisting of England, France and Russia
Battlewagon — battleship
Quisling — a traitor
Blitzkrieg — lightning war
Blood and Guts — George Patton, Jr.
Monty — Field Marshal Sir Bernard Montgomery
Schlieffen Plan — German plan that called for a lightning attack on France through the lowlands of Belgium before Russia could fully mobilize
Desert Fox — Field Marshal Erwin Rommel
Wolf Pack — groups of submarines
Hedgehog — device used on American destroyer escorts to spread depth charges in wide patterns

4) 1 "Dog Tag" card for every participating student made from 3x5-inch colored construction paper.

(Materials list continues on page 170)

5) Paper and pens.

6) Large manila envelope (12x15-inches) for the materials.

PROCEDURE:

1) Divide the students into two evenly matched teams, but each student works individually. Appoint a team captain.

2) 1 "Dog Tag" card is given to each student.

3) The players are told that they are detectives and have many clues to find.

4) Place half of the cards face down on a table in front of each team.

5) Each student chooses a card and uses either a dictionary, encyclopedia, or textbook to find the answer to the term or nickname.

6) When the answer has been found, the term or nickname, the definition, and the number in the lower right-hand corner of the card are recorded on paper.

7) The card is returned to the table and a new one is chosen. The players are to identify as many items accurately as they possibly can within the time allowed.

8) The prepared answer sheet can be used in one of two ways: the team captain of team 1 may check the answers of team 2 members and vice versa, or answers may be checked by the teacher and reported to the students.

9) For each correct answer, a hole is punched on the "Dog Tag" card.

10) At the end of the game, the player with the most holes punched on the "Dog Tag" is declared the best detective and it is assumed that "you were there."

* * *

WORLD COMMUNICATION : FOREIGN LANGUAGES

JUEGO

PURPOSE: To promote a further recognition of counting in Spanish.

GRADE LEVEL: 7th or 8th grade

TIME: 15-20 minutes each round

NUMBER: Small group to an entire class

METHOD OF CHECKING: Teacher

MATERIALS:
1) 1 10x30-inch colored posterboard call sheet for the teacher, marked as below:

J	U	E	G	O
1	1	1	1	1
2	2	2	2	2
3	3	3	3	3
4	4	4	4	4
5	5	5	5	5
6	6	6	6	6
7	7	7	7	7
8	8	8	8	8
9	9	9	9	9
10	10	10	10	10
11	11	11	11	11
12	12	12	12	12
13	13	13	13	13
14	14	14	14	14
15	15	15	15	15
16	16	16	16	16
17	17	17	17	17
18	18	18	18	18
19	19	19	19	19
20	20	20	20	20
30	30	30	30	30
40	40	40	40	40
50	50	50	50	50
60	60	60	60	60
70	70	70	70	70
80	80	80	80	80
90	90	90	90	90
100	100	100	100	100

(Materials list continues on page 174)

2) 140 2x1-inch colored posterboard call tokens, marked as below:

J		G	
	VEINTE		DIEZ Y NUEVE
	(20)		(19)

3) 1 5x6-inch colored posterboard Juego card for every participant: each card should be numbered at random with numbers 1 through 20 and by tens to 100 in numerals.

J	U	E	G	O
6	10	4	7	15
12	3	9	11	10
18	5	16	40	70
20	50	2	80	13
30	8	60	1	90

4) 1 5x6-inch colored posterboard Juego card for every participant: each card should be numbered at random with numbers 1 through 20 and by tens to 100 in Spanish.

J & E G O

DOS	UNO	CUARENTA	CATORCE	TRECE
QUINCE	SESENTA	NUEVE	SEIS	NOVENTA
TREINTA	CIENTO	DIEZ y SEIS	OCHENTA	SIETE
OCHO	VEINTE	SETENTA	UNO	CINCUENTA
DIEZ y SIETE	TRES	CINCO	CUATRO	DOCE

5) 25 plastic tokens, buttons, and so on placed in a letter-sized envelope or cloth pouch.

6) 1 6x9-inch manila envelope for the call tokens.

7) Letter-sized envelopes or cloth pouches.

8) Large manila envelope (18x22-inches) for the materials.

PROCEDURE:

1) Each student is given one Juego card in numerals or Spanish, depending on the version being played, and related materials.

2) The teacher places the call tokens in a box or bowl to use in drawing numbers to call out. If the numeral Juego cards are used, call out the Spanish numbers. If the Spanish Juego cards are used, call out the numbers in English.

3) The teacher draws one call token and reads the letter and number printed on it (for example, "J−20 or G−ochenta," depending on version). Note: the number that appears in the parentheses on each call token is for the Spanish version of Juego.

4) Each player looks at the appropriate row on his or her Juego card (in this case, the row below "J" or "G"). If the correct English or Spanish number (in the example, veinte or 80) appears in that row on the player's card, the player covers it with a plastic token or button.

5) The teacher places the call token in the corresponding space on the call sheet, draws another, and goes through the same procedure.

6) Play continues in this manner until a player covers 5 correct numbers in a row—vertically, horizontally, or diagonally—and calls "Juego" to indicate winning.

(Procedures continue on page 176)

7) Once "Juego" has been called, no other player may place a token or button on his or her card until the original has been checked for accuracy.

8) For accuracy's sake, the winner should read off the numbers covered so that the teacher can check them against the numbers covered on the call sheet.

9) The winning player in each instance is to receive a certain number of points—to be determined by the teacher.

10) Variations of the game include:
   a) Four corners—all four corners must be covered with tokens or buttons to win.
   b) Picture frame—all squares on the outside of the card must be covered with tokens or buttons to win.
   c) Black-out—all squares must be covered with tokens or buttons to win.

* * *

FROM A TO Z

PURPOSE: To assist students in becoming proficient in spelling and in using a Spanish-English dictionary.

GRADE LEVEL: 7th or 8th grade

TIME: 25-40 minutes

NUMBER: 3-5 players per wheel

METHOD OF CHECKING: Self-checking

MATERIALS:
1)   1 Spanish-English dictionary for each participant.

2)   1 alphabet wheel with spinner and all letters of the English alphabet represented.

3)   2 dice.

4)   1 timer.

PROCEDURE:
1)   3-5 players gather around a designated area and are given the appropriate materials.

2)   Appoint one person as the leader—the best student in the group.

3)   The students roll a die to determine the order of play; the player with the highest score begins.

4)   The first player spins the alphabet wheel and rolls the dice. If the spinner lands on "e" and the dice on "10," it would be the player's task to find a Spanish word in the dictionary beginning with "e" having 10 letters. For example: "estudiante."

(Procedures continue on page 178)

5) Set the timer for 1-2 minutes after the wheel is spun.

6) If the word is found within the time limit, the player receives the number of points rolled on the dice or the number of letters in the original word.

7) If the task is not completed within the time limit, any other player in the group may show the leader a word starting with "e" having 10 letters, thereby gaining the points.

8) Play then moves to the player whose turn was coming up next before the volunteer answered.

9) Play continues in this fashion with players alternating turns.

10) The player with the highest score at the end of "time" is the winner.

11) The teacher should circulate around the room to answer any questions or to settle any disputes.

* * *

```
********************************************************************
                            PUZZLER
********************************************************************
```

PURPOSE: To reinforce spelling patterns and the use of a Spanish-English dictionary.

GRADE LEVEL: 7th or 8th grade

TIME: No specific time

NUMBER: From 2 to 30 students, paired

METHOD OF CHECKING: Self-checking with dictionaries

MATERIALS:
1) A large assortment of letters 1-inch square on colored posterboard to be manipulated into words.
2) 1 container for each participant (margarine tub or the round cardboard circle from Scotch brand book tape no. 845 with a circle taped to one end).
3) Cassell's (or similar) Spanish-English dictionaries, 1 for every 2 students.
4) Score paper and pencils.
5) A small cardboard box for the materials.

PROCEDURE:
1) Players are paired (try to match ability levels) and given a variety of letters, two containers, score paper and pencils, and one dictionary.
2) Each player secretly builds a word in Spanish, checks the spelling in the dictionary, mixes it up, places it in the container, and shakes it up.
3) For each round, at the beginning, the players write the word on one side of the paper in case of a challenge.
4) The partners switch containers and each tries to build and guess the other's word.
5) The player who guesses his or her partner's word first scores the number of letters in the word (a seven-letter word guessed correctly would be worth seven points, and so on).
6) A challenge may be issued at any time concerning the correct spelling of the word. If this occurs, the intended word is located in the dictionary and if the spelling is correct, the originator of the word receives the points. If incorrect, the challenger receives the points.
7) When a round is finished, new words are built and the partners trade again.
8) At any time the partners may give clues. For example: "At the count of five we will each say the first letter of the word in the container."
9) The game is over when a certain number of points is reached or a time limit is up. At that time, the partner with the highest score wins.
10) Variations:
    Players throw dice to determine how many letters the word in the container should have.
    or
    Use small words to make scrambled sentences.

* * *

SPAN THE RIVER

PURPOSE: To assist students in learning the different parts of speech that make up a Spanish sentence.

GRADE LEVEL: 7th or 8th grade

TIME: 30-40 minutes

NUMBER: 2-4 players per gameboard

METHOD OF CHECKING: Teacher

MATERIALS:

1) 1 Span the River gameboard per 2-4 players. Gameboards can be made from 14x22-inch colored posterboard.

❧ SPAN THE RIVER ❧

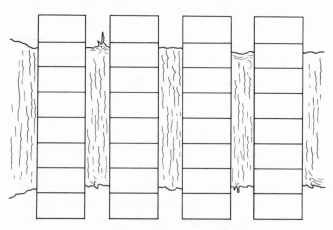

❧ THE GUADALQUIVIR RIVER ❧

2) 50 1x2-inch colored posterboard cards bearing the different parts of speech. For example:

Nouns	Pronouns	Adjectives	Verbs
España	yo	bonito	comprar
Carlos	tú	nuevo	estar
Luisa	él	pocos	entrar
puente	ella	viejo	decir
pueblo	Ud.	azul	recibir
Tejas	nosotros	muchos	vender
el niño	vosotros	alto(s)	comer
la hermana	ellos	inglés (es)	ser
el mapa	ellas	inglesa(s)	ir
la mano	Uds.	grande(s)	escribir
las mujeres		español(es)	pasar
los lápices		española(s)	
la ciudad		tres	
el hombre		diez	

Prepositions	Adverbs	Conjunctions	Articles
de	cerca	aunque	el
desde	lejos	porque	los
a	muy	pero	la
sobre	claramente	si	las
por	fácilmente	o	un
para	más	y	una
con	aquí		
en	allí		
sin	bien		

If more than one set of cards is desired, use as many different words as possible.

3) Scrap paper and pencils.

4) 1 die.

5) Large manila envelope (16x20-inches) for the materials.

PROCEDURE:

1) 2-4 players gather around a table and are given a Span the River gameboard, a set of cards, scrap paper, and pencils.

2) Each player throws the die; the player with the highest number goes first. (Play goes to the right around the circle until the original player starts again.)

3) The first player deals out two cards to each person and the remainder of the deck is placed face down near the gaming area.

4) The two cards are placed anywhere on a player's bridge and are later to become part of a sentence.

5) During the first round, players may only choose a card from the pile face down. The card that is chosen may either be placed on the bridge or discarded to begin a discard pile.

6) In round two and each succeeding round, a player may:
   a) choose a card from the deck face down, or
   b) choose any card from the discard pile, or
   c) ask anyone in the circle for a card to fit into the sentence, provided that the player also has a card that is useful to the player asked (in other words, players should only trade useful cards), or
   d) move two cards around on the bridge to begin the formation of a sentence.

7) Scrap paper may be used to help a player form a sentence.

8) When a verb is chosen for use in the sentence, it should be conjugated to fit the mood of the sentence.

9) When a player has covered all sections of a bridge and a proper sentence has been formed, he or she raises a hand to indicate that the sentence is ready for checking by the teacher.

10) If the sentence is correct, the player scores 8 points (1 point for each section). The remaining players score 1 point for each card correctly placed toward a complete sentence.

11) If the sentence is incorrect, play resumes until another player indicates a complete sentence.

12) The game is over when one or more players have correctly fashioned a sentence or time is called.

* * *

****
ARCHITECTURAL OLD MAID
****

PURPOSE: To familiarize students with buildings that are famous architectural and historical sites in Spain.

GRADE LEVEL: 7th or 8th grade

TIME: 25 minutes

NUMBER: 3-4 players for each deck of cards

METHOD OF CHECKING: Self-checking

MATERIALS:
1)   1 set of 3x4-inch white posterboard cards, for every 3-4 players; 51 cards to a set. Cards should bear reproductions of famous architectural buildings or sites in matching pairs. There should be one identified odd card for each set. Some famous architectural buildings and sites are:

el Alcázar — Segovia
el Prado — Madrid
la Alhambra — Granada
el Escorial — northwest of Madrid
La Cathedral de Santa Maria — Burgos
Church of the Sacred Family — Barcelona
La Valle de Los Caídos — northwest of Madrid
Monastery of San Jerónimo — Granada
Roman Theater — Mérida
Great Mosque of Córdoba — Córdoba
La Casa de las Conchas — Salamanca
San Esteban — Salamanca

If more than one set is desired and if it is possible, change the buildings to cover more architectural sites.

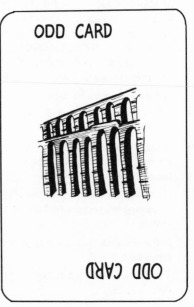

2) Large manila envelope (12x15-inches) for the materials.

PROCEDURE:

1) 3-4 students gather around a table and one is appointed dealer.

2) Dealer shuffles the cards and distributes them, one at a time, until the pack is exhausted.

3) It does not matter if every player does not receive the same number of cards.

4) Players match pairs and place the cards face-down in front of them, without showing them to the other players.

5) All the cards laid out in this manner are left in front of the player, in order to discover errors, if any.

6) After players have discarded their pairs, the dealer begins by spreading the remaining cards, like a fan, and allows his or her left-hand neighbor to draw one card at random.

7) The card so drawn is examined, and if it completes a pair, the two cards are discarded.

8) Whether it forms a pair or not, the second player's cards are spread and presented to the next player on the left, to be drawn from in the same manner.

9) This process of drawing, forming pairs, and discarding is continued until it is found that one player remains with one card.

10) This card is of course the "odd card," and the unfortunate holder of it is the Architectural Old Maid, but only for that deal.

* * *

```
*****************************************************************
```
CLASSIFICATION SEARCH
```
*****************************************************************
```

PURPOSE: To aid students in becoming competent in spelling Spanish words, using a Spanish-English dictionary, understanding a definition, and building a Spanish sentence.

GRADE LEVEL: 7th or 8th grade

TIME: 25-40 minutes

NUMBER: 4-6 players per group

METHOD OF CHECKING: Teacher

MATERIALS:
1) 1 Spanish-English dictionary for each participant.

2) 4-inch wooden cubes that have "animals," "places," "events," "objects," etc. on the six sides; 1 per group.

3) 4-inch wooden cubes that have the numbers 4, 5, 6, 7, 8, and 9 on the six sides; 1 per group.

4) 1 timer.

PROCEDURE:
1) 4-6 players form a small circle on the floor, appoint a captain, and are given the appropriate materials.

2) The student appointed as captain goes first and rolls both the wooden cube with the categories and the wooden cube with the numbers.

3) If the category cube turns up with "place" and the number cube with "6," the player must locate a place in the dictionary containing 6 letters. For example: Madrid.

4) The player then makes up a sentence using the word so that the group is aware that the definition was understood. For example: Madrid es la capital de España.

5) Set the timer for 4-5 minutes after the cubes have been rolled.

6) If the word is found and a sentence completed within the time limit, the player receives the number of points rolled on the cube.

7) If the answer is incorrect, anyone in the circle may answer and score the points.

8) Play resumes with the student who correctly found a word and built a sentence rolling the cubes to start another round.

9) When a word is found and a sentence formed, the teacher should be consulted to verify that all is correct.

10) Play continues until everyone has had two turns or time is called.

11) At the end, the student with the most points is the winner.

* * *

****
MAP MARATHON
****

PURPOSE: To aid in the comprehension of Spanish geography and history.

GRADE LEVEL: 7th or 8th grade

TIME: 30-45 minutes

NUMBER: 3-5 players per gameboard

METHOD OF CHECKING: Answer sheet

MATERIALS:

1) 2 transparencies—1 containing the map of Spain with cities, rivers, and mountain ranges, and the other containing the paths the players must travel. Sample paths are included on the illustration below. Draw with a Sharpie® or similar pen for permanency.

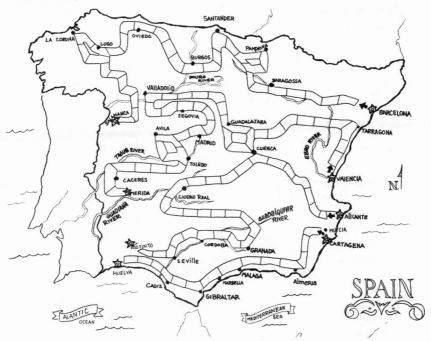

2) 30 3x5-inch index cards bearing questions concerning geographical and historical terms and sites; one-half in English and one-half in Spanish. Number them 1-30 in the lower right-hand corner. For example:

Name the famous mountains that separate Spain from France. (Pyrenees)
Which mountain range is known as the "snowy range"? (Sierra Nevadas)
Which city is Spain's major port on the Atlantic? (Cádiz)
Name two famous resorts of the Costa del Sol. (Torremolinos and Marbella)
Which city is the capital of Spain? (Madrid)
Traduzca La Valle de los Caídos en inglés. (The Valley of the Fallen)
Who built the Royal Monastery of San Lorenzo del Escorial? (Philipe Segundo)
What is Avila famous for? (one of the great religious centers)
Traduzca: "Toledo fué la Ciudad Imperial y Coronado." (Toledo was the imperial and crowned city)

(Materials list continues on page 186)

Which city has a well-preserved Roman aqueduct? (Segovia)
Which city has the reputation of being Spain's most European city? (Barcelona)
Which city is connected by the Guadalquivir River and a canal to the Atlantic
Ocean and is a manufacturing center for armaments and tobacco? (Seville)
What is the more famous name for Rodrigo Díaz de Vivar? (El Cid)
Which city has the famous Moorish building, "La Alhambra"? (Granada)

If more than one set of cards is desired, change the questions so that students become more familiar with Spain's geography and history.

3) 1 master list of questions and answers per gameboard dry-mounted to a piece of colored posterboard. List the questions and answers according to the number on the cards (*see* number 2).

4) 1 die.

5) 4 Vis-A-Vis® markers in different colors.

6) Damp paper towels.

7) Overhead projector and screen.

8) 1 timer.

9) Large manila envelope (12x15-inches) for the materials.

PROCEDURE:

1) Appoint one player as leader who will possess the answer sheet, draw the lines in the maze, and set the timer.

2) Remaining players are to form a semicircle facing the screen with the cards placed face down in the middle.

3) Each player rolls the die to determine what his or her starting city will be:

Barcelona — highest
Valencia — second highest
Alicante — third highest
Cartagena — lowest

Ahead of time, assign the color that goes with each city.

4) The object is to travel across the country by answering the questions and coming out on the opposite side of the map in the "sister" city.

Barcelona — Salamanca
Valencia — Merida
Alicante — Ríotinto
Cartagena — Huelva

5) The player who represents Barcelona starts by drawing a card. If the card is in English, the question must be answered. If the card is in Spanish, the question must be translated. If correct, the leader connects two spaces on the player's path and the player retains the card. If incorrect, no forward progress is made, and once into the game one space is lost for each wrong answer and the card is placed at the bottom of the pile.

6) Players alternate turns following the same procedures until one arrives at the "sister" city.

7) When the game is over, each card in Spanish is worth two points and each one in English is worth one point. The player to reach the sister city first adds an extra five points to his or her score.

8) The player with the highest score is the winner.

* * *

PRENDAS

PURPOSE: To help students to think and to follow simple directions in Spanish.

GRADE LEVEL: 7th or 8th grade

TIME: 45 minutes

NUMBER: Small group to an entire class

METHOD OF CHECKING: Teacher

MATERIALS:
1) Articles belonging to students (pens, pencils, piece of clothing, piece of jewelry, and so on).

2) 40 3x5-inch index cards on which have been written or typed in Spanish simple tasks to be performed. On the back of the cards, give the English translation. For example:

   Conte a veinte en uno minuto.
   Diga un cuento en cuatro minutos.
   Escriba una carta corta en tres minutos.
   Tome un libro y leyá un párrafo corto en dos minutos.
   Traduzca un frase de Español en Inglés en uno minuto.

3) 2 desk chairs.

4) 1 timer.

5) Large manila envelope (10x13-inches) for the materials.

PROCEDURE:
1) Each player adds a piece of clothing, jewelry, pen or pencil, and so on to a pile.

2) One player is chosen to be the judge and another is chosen to be the guard.

3) The students are to form a large circle around the judge and guard.

4) Place two chairs back-to-back inside the circle; the guard sits in one and the judge in the other so that he or she cannot see what the guard is holding over his or her head.

5) The instruction or command cards are placed face down on the desk in front of the judge.

6) The player who is the guard chooses an item from the pile.

7) The player who owns the item chosen is now called "el prisionero—the prisoner."

8) The guard holds the item over the judge's head and may say: "¿Qué tiene que hacer el prisionero para reclamado?" ("What must the prisoner do to redeem this?")

9) The judge then sentences the prisoner to perform a task by choosing a card from the pile and reading the directions in Spanish.

10) Set the timer for the amount of time indicated on the card.

11) The prisoner must carry out the sentence within the required time allotment or forfeit the turn.

12) The teacher judges whether the sentence is being performed correctly and may award points for how well it is carried out.

(Procedures continue on page 188)

13) The game continues until each player has had a chance to be sentenced, to perform the sentence, and to retrieve the forfeit.

14) If time runs out before everyone has had a turn, play may be continued another day.

15) The items still not claimed may be held for ransom or returned—the class and the teacher decide.

* * *

MIENTES TÚ

PURPOSE: To assist students in the study of names of fruits and vegetables to be used in a game of progression, memory, listening, and sentence building.

GRADE LEVEL: 8th grade

TIME: 30-45 minutes

NUMBER: Small group to an entire class

METHOD OF CHECKING: Self-checking and teacher

MATERIALS:

1) 1 1x2-inch colored posterboard card bearing the name of a fruit or vegetable for each player. For example:

el tomate = tomato	la naranja = orange
la patata = potato	el limón = lemon
el betabel = beet	la manzana = apple
la calabaza = pumpkin	la fresa = strawberry
el boniato = sweet potato	el plátano = banana

2) 20-30 3x3-inch colored posterboard cards bearing directions for tricks. For example:

Ladra como un perro — Bark like a dog.
Maulla como un gato — Meow like a cat.
Canta como un gallo — Sing like a rooster.
Chifla como un tren — Whistle like a train.
Brinca como un chivo — Jump like a goat.
Vuela como un pájaro — Fly like a bird.

3) 2 10x13-inch manila envelopes; one marked "fruits and vegetables," the other "tricks."

4) 2 master lists — one with fruits and vegetables in Spanish and English and one with the tricks in Spanish and English.

5) 1 Spanish-English dictionary for each participant.

PROCEDURE:

1) All players are to sit in a circle.

2) Appoint one player to hold the "fruits and vegetables" envelope and one to hold the "tricks" envelope.

3) The player with the "fruits and vegetables" envelope walks around the circle while each player picks a card in order to find his or her identity for the game.

4) Players may or may not look up their identities in the dictionary. They will, however, need to identify themselves when called upon.

5) One player is assigned to start the game. The player may say, "Anoche ví al Señor Limón en la panadería de la esquina." (Last night I saw Mr. Lemon in the bakery on the corner.)

6) The player whose name is Limón says, "Mientes tú." ("You fib.")
"¿Dónde estabas tú?" ("Where were you?"), asks the first player.
"Yo estaba en la bodega de la Señora Patata" ("I was in Mrs. Potato's grocery"), the second player may reply.

(Procedures continue on page 190)

7) Now the player whose name is Patata says, "Mientes tú." ("You fib.") "¿Dónde estabas tú?" ("Where were you?"), asks Señor Limón or Señora Patata. "Yo estaba en la casa del Señor Betabel" ("I was in Mr. Beet's House"), Señora Patata may reply.

8) The game continues rapidly around the circle with each player identifying his or her vegetable or fruit when called upon and giving a reply sentence telling where he or she was last night.

9) The student with the master list of "fruits and vegetables" indicates whether a player has correctly identified himself or herself, and the teacher indicates whether the sentence is correct.

10) A forfeit occurs when, 1) incorrect identification is made, 2) an incorrect sentence is given, or 3) no reply is made.

11) To pay a forfeit means that the player who does not respond correctly must give on deposit something that belongs to him or her, such as a pen, book, or ring.

12) Then the game begins again following the same procedure as outlined above.

13) When it is decided to end the game, the player with the "tricks" envelope goes up to the players who have paid a forfeit, each of whom must choose a card from the envelope.

14) The players must perform the tricks in order to redeem their belongings. The student with the master list of tricks judges whether the trick is carried out correctly.

15) If correct, the item is given back to the owner. If incorrect, the class and teacher may decide to return the item or to keep it for another chance later.

* * *

```
*****************************************************************
```
INCORPORATION
```
*****************************************************************
```

PURPOSE: To acquaint students with the many French words that have been incorporated into the English language.

GRADE LEVEL: 7th or 8th grade

TIME: 30 minutes

NUMBER: Form A—2-4 players; Form B—entire class

METHOD OF CHECKING: Teacher

MATERIALS:

1) French dictionaries, French textbooks, language books, and other sources.

2) Paper and pencils for each student.

PROCEDURE:

Prior to playing the game, the teacher should present some words and definitions that have been assimilated into the English language. For example:

au gratin	café	croissant
au jus	cartouche	fête
au lait	carte blanche	gaffe
beau monde	chignon	garni
bisque	cloisonné	gazette
bivouac	coiffeur	laissez-faire
boutique	connoisseur	lamé
boutonniere	cordon bleu	noël
bravo	corps de ballet	papier-mâché
brochette	cravat	vichyssoise

Form A

1) Two teams of students are formed.

2) Teams race for 15 minutes listing as many French words incorporated into the English language as possible. Dictionaries, language books, French texts, and other sources in the media center may be consulted.

3) The team with the most correct words wins. (It is advisable to have teams come together for a discussion and to check the words.)

Form B

1) A list of words is presented to the class by the teacher.

2) The class works as individuals attempting to recall and list as many words as possible.

3) The student with the most words that are spelled correctly wins.

* * *

LE DESTIN

PURPOSE: To provide practice in learning French phrases and numbers.

GRADE LEVEL: 7th or 8th grade

TIME: 30 minutes

NUMBER: 4 players per pack of cards

METHOD OF CHECKING: Self-checking

MATERIALS:

1) 1 pack of Le Destin cards made up of 54 3x4-inch colored posterboard cards bearing phrases and numbers with 4 wild Le Destin cards. Each set can be of a different color for ease in sorting. For example:

un N'est-ce pas?	1 Isn't it so?
(5 each)	(5 each)

deux Gardez la foi.	2 Keep the faith.
(5 each)	(5 each)

trois

Je suis pret.

(5 each)

3

I am ready.

(5 each)

quatre

Tout de suite!

(5 each)

4

immediately!

(5 each)

cinq

C'est la vie.

(5 each)

5

That's life.

(5 each)

(Materials list continues on page 194)

(4 each)

2) Paper and pencils for each player.

3) Rubber bands to band the packs of cards together.

4) Large manila envelope (12x15-inches) for the materials.

PROCEDURE:

1) Players sit at a table. The dealer shuffles the cards and deals 5 cards to each player.

2) The remainder of the cards are placed face down to form a draw pile.

3) The top card is turned face up and placed next to the draw pile. (If it is a Le Destin card, the draw cards are reshuffled and another card is drawn.)

4) The player on the dealer's left begins by trying to match the face up card by number *or* phrase. For example: "1" may be played on "un" and "N'est-ce pas?" may be played on "Isn't it so?" When matching a card, the player must translate the number and phrase. (If written in English, the player must give the French translation and vice versa.)

5) If a player cannot translate the number or the phrase, the card may not be played and the next player takes a turn.

6) Le Destin cards are wild and may be played on any card and players do not have to translate. When someone plays a Le Destin card, the player announces the next phrase or number to be played.

7) A player who cannot match a card or play a Le Destin card, draws from the pile until he or she can play. When the pile is used up, a player passes if a match cannot be made.

8) Play rotates clockwise. The hand is over when any player is out of cards or when no one can play.

9) Players add up all the points of the cards still held, counting each at face value with a Le Destin card worth 20 points.

10) The player with the lowest total score after 3 hands wins.

11) NOTE: Each pack of cards should contain 5 different phrases and 5 different numbers to give players additional practice by exchanging packs of cards.

* * *

MÉMOIRE

PURPOSE: To provide practice in the recognition of French words.

GRADE LEVEL: 7th or 8th grade

TIME: 25 minutes

NUMBER: 4-6 players per deck

METHOD OF CHECKING: Self-checking

MATERIALS:

1) 44 3x4-inch colored posterboard cards bearing the following:

la femme (l' épouse)	wife
la fille	daughter
le fil	son
le frère	brother
grand-mère	grandmother
grand-père	grandfather
le mari (l' époux)	husband
la mère	mother
le père	father
petite-fille	granddaughter
petit-fils	grandson
la soleur	sister
le beau-fils	son-in-law, stepson
la belle-fille	sister-in-law, stepsister
la belle-mère	mother-in-law, stepmother
le beau-père	father-in-law, stepfather
le cousin (e)	cousin
le gendre	son-in-law
le neveu	nephew
la nièce	niece
l' oncle	uncle
la tante	aunt

2) Large manila envelope (12x15-inches) for the materials.

PROCEDURE:

1) Four to six players gather around a table or in a circle on the floor in alphabetical order.

2) The student with the last initial closest to the beginning of the alphabet is the dealer.

3) The dealer shuffles the cards and places them face down on the table or floor. The cards may be laid out in any pattern, but no two cards should touch each other.

4) Each player will want to remember the position of each card as it is turned up on the table or floor, since this will help in building pairs.

5) The dealer starts the game by turning face up any two cards, one at a time. All players look at the two cards as they are turned up, but the two cards are not immediately picked up, just turned face up.

6) If the two cards are a pair, the dealer picks them up, keeps them, and turns up two more cards. A pair consists of the French word and its English translation. For

(Procedures continue on page 196)

example: la fille—daughter. The dealer's turn continues as long as he or she turns up pairs.

7) If the two cards are not a pair, they are turned face down again and left in their original places. This ends the dealer's turn. (Cards are picked up only when they are a pair.)

8) After the dealer's turn is over, the player to the left of the dealer continues the game. Play continues around the table or circle on the floor to the left.

9) The winner is the player who has accumulated the greatest number of correct pairs after all of the cards have been picked up from the table or floor.

10) Each player scores one point for each pair held at the end of the game.

11) Variations: Instead of proper nouns, substitute months and days of the week, time, or numbers.

* * *

BATTRE LA MESURE

PURPOSE: To help students gain proficiency in recognizing time in French.

GRADE LEVEL: 7th or 8th grade

TIME: 30 minutes

NUMBER: Forms A & B—entire class; Form C—2 students

METHOD OF CHECKING: Teacher and/or answer sheet

MATERIALS:
1) 2 clock faces with moveable hands, and chalkboard.

2) 50 3x5-inch index cards bearing different times such as 3:05.

3) Answer sheet dry-mounted to a piece of colored posterboard. For example:

    10:45—dix heures quarante-cinq
    1:20—un heure vingt
    3:05—trois heures cinq
    7:57—sept heures cinquante-sept
    8:23—huit heures vingt-trois
    6:52—six heures cinquante-deux
    2:36—deux heures trente-six
    11:12—onze heures douze
    1:18—un heure dix-huit
    4:37—quatre heures trente-sept
    5:39—cinq heures trente-neuf
    7:04—sept heures quarte
    2:14—deux heures quartorze
    9:34—neuf heures trente-quatre
    6:43—six heures quarante-trois
    4:22—quatre heures vingt-deux
    12:01—douze heures un
    1:53—un heure cinquante-trois
    2:22—deux heures vingt-deux
    8:09—huit heures neuf

4) Pencil and paper for scoring.

5) Large manila envelope (12x15-inches) for the materials.

PROCEDURE:
    Form A
1) The class is divided into two teams. The clocks are placed in a chalk rail with the players facing the chalkboard in relay fashion.

2) The teacher draws 1 card and reads the time in French. (A student may also be chosen to do this.)

3) The first player on each team walks to a clock, fixes the hands at the correct time, and raises a hand when finished.

4) The teacher calls on the first player to raise a hand. The first player to get the time correct must also answer with a sentence in French containing the time indicated on the clock. If the first player is incorrect, the second player has a chance to gain a

(Procedures continue on page 198)

point by answering correctly. If neither player is correct, the teacher gives the correct answer and no points are scored.

5) The teams continue in this fashion, receiving a point for each correct answer.

6) The team with the most points wins.

Form B
The same a Form A except it is played as a relay with the cards divided into 2 sets. Each player chooses a card and races, in turn, to set the correct time on the clock. The first team finished wins.

Form C
Played the same as Form A but with only 2 students who race each other for points. A third student acts as referee and scorekeeper, using the answer sheet to check answers.

* * *

JETON

PURPOSE: To promote familiarity with French vocabulary words.

GRADE LEVEL: 7th or 8th grade

TIME: 40 minutes

NUMBER: 1 per gameboard in small groups (4) to an entire class

METHOD OF CHECKING: Caller

MATERIALS:

1) Jeton gameboards made from 9x12-inch tagboard bearing French vocabulary words; 1 gameboard for each player. Vocabulary words should be placed in random order and each card should be different.

J E T O N

PARLE	BEAUCOUP	TOUJOUR	BIEN	QUELLE
L'ÉCOLE	QUI	TROUVE	POURQUOI	VOILÀ
AVEC	ENTREZ		COMBIEN	il
QUELLE	POR VOUS	L'ÉCOLE	JE	VOUS
BIEN	AVEC	QUI	DIT	BEAUCOUP

2) 25 tokens per player.

3) A letter-sized envelope or cloth pouch for each set of tokens.

4) Master list of words dry-mounted to a piece of color posterboard to be used by the caller as a check sheet.

5) 80 3x4-inch colored posterboard cards bearing one of the letters in "jeton" and a French vocabulary word.

(Illustration appears on page 200)

```
┌─────────────────────────┐   ┌─────────────────────────┐
│ J                       │   │ T                       │
│                         │   │                         │
│         Vous            │   │        Combien          │
│                         │   │                         │
│                         │   │                         │
└─────────────────────────┘   └─────────────────────────┘
```

6) Large manila envelope (16x20-inches) for the materials.

PROCEDURE:

1) Each student is given one Jeton card and related materials.

2) Appoint one student to be the caller.

3) The caller draws one of the 80 cards, calls out the letter and word, and marks the answer with a token on the master sheet.

4) Players locate that word under the letter called, and place a token to cover the appropriate space. The word can be covered only if it appears in the column under the called letter.

5) The first player to cover five spaces horizontally, vertically or diagonally calls out, "Jeton!"

6) Once "Jeton" has been called, no other player may place a token on his or her card until the original has been checked for accuracy.

7) The caller verifies the winning card by checking against the master sheet.

8) Players clear their cards and trade with their neighbors, and play begins again.

9) Variations of the game include:
   a) Four corners—all four corners must be covered with tokens to win.
   b) Picture frame—all squares on the outside of the card must be covered with tokens to win.
   c) Black-out—all squares must be covered with tokens to win.

* * *

```
*****************************************************************
```
ALIGNER
```
*****************************************************************
```

PURPOSE: To provide practice in translating sentences from French to English.

GRADE LEVEL: 7th or 8th grade

TIME: 25 minutes

NUMBER: 2 players per gameboard

METHOD OF CHECKING: Answer sheet

MATERIALS:
1) 1 checkerboard for every 2 students.

2) 10 checkers (5 red, 5 black).

3) 30 3x4-inch colored posterboard cards bearing sentences in French. For example:

J'ai préparé ma leçon pour lundi. (a)
Où se trove l'Amerique? (b)
J'aime ma soeur. (c)
Qu'est-ce que vous étudiez? (d)
Le crayon est sur le table. (e)

Note: Include the letter of the sentence on the card and answer sheet for ease in checking.

4) Answer sheet with the English translations for the sentences dry-mounted to a piece of colored posterboard.

5) Large manila envelope (16x20-inches) for the materials.

PROCEDURE:
1) Players are given the checkerboard and other Aligner materials, and they determine the order of play.

2) Cards are shuffled and placed face down to one side of the checkerboard.

3) The first player draws a card, reads the sentence in French, gives the English translation and places the card at the bottom of the pile. The opposing player may use the answer sheet to verify a correct answer.

4) If correct, the player may place a checker anywhere on the board. If incorrect, no checkers are placed on the board and the other player takes a turn.

5) Play continues with players alternating turns until one player has all 5 checkers arranged in a line, horizontally, vertically or diagnonally.

6) The first player to form a line of 5 wins.

* * *

LES PAGES JAUNES

PURPOSE: To provide practice in translating English into French and to use the French yellow pages.

GRADE LEVEL: 7th or 8th grade

TIME: 35 minutes

NUMBER: 2 students per group

METHOD OF CHECKING: Answer sheet

MATERIALS:

1) 2 yellow pages in French per group.

2) French-English dictionary.

3) French-English textbook.

4) Clock, stopwatch, or timer.

5) 2 Vis-A-Vis® pens.

6) Damp paper towels to wipe cards clean.

7) 2 Les Pages Jaunes cards of 9x12-inch tagboard bearing 10 short paragraphs in English such as:

Help! The pipe under the sink burst. The plumbers name and telephone number are
_____.

My tooth aches. Call the dentist.
        Name: _____
        Telephone #: _____

The dog needs a shot. Which vet do you recommend?
        Name: _____
        Telephone #: _____

The roof is leaking. What roofer shall I call?
        Name: _____
        Telephone #: _____

Call a taxi. It's time to go home.
        Name: _____
        Telephone #: _____

Leave space between paragraphs for the translations.

8) Answer sheet with paragraphs written in French dry-mounted to a piece of colored posterboard.

9) Large manila envelope (12x15-inches) for the materials.

PROCEDURE:

1) Two players are each given a Les Pages Jaune card, the French yellow pages, and a Vis-A-Vis® pen. French language texts and French-English dictionaries should be readily accessible.

2) Players have 25 minutes to translate the paragraphs and use the yellow pages to include names and telephone numbers.

3) After 20 minutes, the boards are checked with the answer sheet.

4) The player with the most paragraphs translated correctly wins.

5) Note: Request for a telephone book in French should be addressed to your local telephone company business office. From there, the service representative will have you fill out a form and will send it to the office in Montreal. Once they receive the telephone book requested, they will mail it to you and charge you through your next phone bill.

* * *

```
*****************************************************************
```
DÉPASSER
```
*****************************************************************
```

PURPOSE: To allow students to compose a paragraph in French using as many business sources as possible from the French yellow pages.

GRADE LEVEL: 7th or 8th grade

TIME: 40 minutes

NUMBER: 4 students

METHOD OF CHECKING: Teacher

MATERIALS:
1) 2 French yellow pages.

2) French-English dictionary.

3) French language texts.

4) Paper and pencils.

5) Clock or watch.

6) 4 3x5-inch cards bearing the following instructions:

   You are planning a trip overseas. Write your plans and include as many businesses as possible that you might contact as you make plans.

   You are getting married. Write your wedding plans and include as many businesses as possible that you might need to contact as you make plans.

   You are building a house. Write your construction plans and include as many businesses as possible that you might need to contact as you make plans.

   You are planning a surprise birthday party. Write your birthday plans and include as many businesses as possible that you might need to make plans.

PROCEDURE:
1) The students are divided into two teams and each team draws a card.

2) Using the materials listed, the teams have 30 minutes to write a paragraph in French telling plans and businesses to be contacted. For example: Trip—travel agent, bus line, train station, airport, rental car agency, bank, hotel, luggage shop, and so on.

3) After 30 minutes, teams share paragraphs aloud with the class.

4) The team listing the most businesses from the yellow pages wins.

* * *

SPECULATE

PURPOSE: To promote familiarity with art vocabulary.

GRADE LEVEL: 7th or 8th grade

TIME: 30 minutes

NUMBER: 2 students

METHOD OF CHECKING: Self-checking

MATERIALS:

1) 2 lists of art vocabulary with definitions dry-mounted to a piece of colored poster-board. Some examples are:

abstract — emphasizing lines and colors: generalized or in geometrical forms.
aesthetic — pertaining to a sense of the beautiful.
baroque — extravagantly ornamented style of art and architecture developed during the 17th century.
bas-relief — relief sculpture in which figurines project slightly from the background.
block print — design printed by means of blocks of wood or metal.
calligraphy — lines resembling letter forms produced with a brush.
cartoon — sketch or drawing satirizing or caricaturing something.
ceramics — art and technology of making objects of clay and similar materials treated by firing.
collage — composing a work of art by pasting on a single surface various materials not normally associated with one another, such as newspaper clippings, theater tickets, cloth, and so on.
contemporary — belonging to the same time.
decorative — serving only to decorate in contrast to providing a meaningful experience.
dome — shaped like a hemisphere or inverted bowl.
engrave — to mark or ornament with incised letters or designs.
etch — to cut, bite, or corrode with an acid or the like.
fresco — technique of painting on a moist, lime plaster surface.
genre — paintings in which scenes of everyday life form the subject matter.
glaze — to cover with a thin layer of transparent color in order to modify the tone.
intensity — the strength or sharpness of a color.
mobile — piece of sculpture having delicately balanced units.
mosaic — decoration made of small pieces of inlaid stone, glass, etc.
mural — executed on or afixed to a wall.
opaque — not transparent or translucent.
perspective — technique of depicting volumes and spatial relationships on a flat surface.
pigment — a coloring matter.
primitive — an artist of a preliterate culture; a naive or unschooled artist.
prints — reproductions.
relief — giving appearance of a third dimension.
Renaissance — great revival of art from the 14th to the 17th century.
rococo — style of architecture and decoration originating in France about 1720.
silk screen — print making technique.
tempera — technique of painting.
texture — characteristic visual and tactile quality.
traditional — pertaining to older styles.
water color — technique of painting with paint and water.

(Materials list continues on page 208)

2) Pencil and paper for each player.

3) Large manila envelope (12x15-inches) for the materials.

PROCEDURE:

1) Players determine order of play and each is given a vocabulary list, paper and pencil. Players are seated across the table from one another in order not to see each other's paper.

2) The first player writes a word chosen from the vocabulary list.

3) The second player writes a word from the vocabulary list and tells the first player.

4) The first player tells what letters from that word are found in the word that he or she has chosen.

5) The second player records the matching letters and chooses another word.

6) The first player tells what letters from that word are found in the word that he or she has chosen.

7) Play continues in this manner until the second player guesses the word chosen or has made 10 incorrect guesses.

8) If the player guesses the word in 10 attempts or less, the definition must be given and the player receives 10 points. If the player does not guess the word, the opponent reads the word and its definition and receives 5 points.

9) Play continues with players alternating turns.

10) The winner is the player with the most points after 30 minutes of play.

* * *

ART CHARADES

PURPOSE: To provide students with some familiarity with famous art titles and/or artists.

GRADE LEVEL: 7th or 8th grade

TIME: 30 minutes

NUMBER: Small groups (4) to an entire class

METHOD OF CHECKING: Self-checking

MATERIALS:

1) 30 3x5-inch index cards bearing art titles such as:

"The Night Watch" (Rembrandt)
"The Girl with the Red Hat" (Jan Vermeer van Delft)
"Kitchen Still Life" (Chardin)
"Snow Storm" (Turner)
"Arrangement in Black and Gray" (Whistler)
"The River" (Monet)
"Prima Ballerina" (Degas)
"Fruit Bowl, Glass, and Apples" (Cezanne)
"The Card Players" (Cezanne)
"Starry Night" (Van Gogh)
"The Sleeping Gypsy" (Rousseau)
"The Old Guitarist" (Picasso)
"The Old Clown" (Rouault)
"The Dream" (Beckman)
"Brooklyn Bridge" (Stella)
"I and the Village" (Chagall)
"The Musicians" (Picasso)
"Flowering Trees" (Mondrian)
"Mona Lisa" (Da Vinci)
"Head of a Youth" (Raphael)
"View of Toledo" (El Greco)
"Back from the Market" (Chardin)
"Lady with a Fan" (Picasso)
"The Boating Party" (Cassatt)
"Behind the Scenes" (Degas)
"Four Dancers" (Degas)
"Picking Flowers" (Renoir)
"The Bullfight" (Goya)
"Seascape" (Gainsborough)
"Christina's World" (Wyeth)

2) A stopwatch or clock or watch with a second hand.

3) Chalkboard, chalk, and eraser.

4) A large manila envelope (10x13-inches) for the materials.

PROCEDURE:

Form A

1) The group is divided into two teams and captains are chosen. The captains act as timekeepers and scorekeepers.

(Procedures continue on page 210)

2) Teams determine the order of play and are seated together with one team on one side of the room and the other team on the other side of the room, facing a chalkboard. Cards are placed face down in a pile on a table in front of the teams, as in the diagram below.

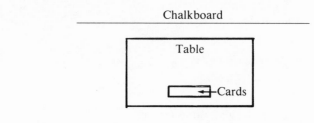

Chalkboard

Table

Cards

Team 1				Team 2		
X	X	X		X	X	X
X	X	X		X	X	X

3) The first player draws a card, reads it silently and places it in a discard pile on the table.

4) The player has 3 minutes to make drawings on the board to give clues as to the words in the art title. (The players may or may not name the artist according to teacher preference.) The player may *not* draw a facsimile of the art piece. Players may use the gestures such as, "sounds like," "small word," and so on, that are used in charades.

5) If team 1 guesses the art title within 3 minutes, 5 points are scored. If the title is not identified, no points are scored and team 2 takes a turn. If a dispute arises, the media specialist or teacher acts as arbitrator.

6) Teams alternate turns for 30 minutes.

7) The team with the most points wins.

Form B
Played the same as Form A with the addition that reproductions are hung around the room and the team member identifying the title also points out the reproduction matching the title for an additional 5 points.

* * *

HEADS ON!

PURPOSE: To help students become more proficient at discerning details.

GRADE LEVEL: 7th or 8th grade

TIME: 15 minutes

NUMBER: 1 student for each set of 8 figures

METHOD OF CHECKING: Self-checking

MATERIALS:
1) 2 Heads On! gameboards (8 figures each) made from 11x17-inch colored posterboard.

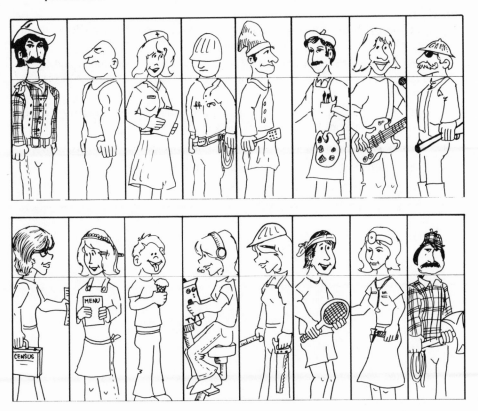

2) Large manila envelope (16x20-inches) for the materials.

PROCEDURE:
1) Divide the figures on the gameboards and separate the heads from the bodies.

2) Two players are each given 8 Heads On! bodies and the matching heads.

3) The players race to match the heads to the correct bodies.

4) The first player to match all the heads to the correct bodies wins.

* * *

```
**********************************************************
```
SWITCH
```
**********************************************************
```

PURPOSE: To help students acquire and/or refine observational skills and become aware of details.

GRADE LEVEL: 7th or 8th grade

TIME: 40 minutes

NUMBER: Small groups to the entire class

METHOD OF CHECKING: Self-checking

MATERIALS:
1) Pencil and paper.

PROCEDURE:
1) The group is divided into two teams and captains are chosen. Captains determine the order of play.

2) Team 1 leaves the room after taking a good look around the room, and team 2 changes and/or switches items in the room. The captain of team 2 records the changes.

3) After 5 minutes, the first team returns and has 10 minutes to find all the changes. The captain of team 1 records the changes found.

4) After 10 minutes, the captains compare lists and changes not found are revealed.

5) Steps 2 through 4 are repeated with team 2 leaving the room.

6) The team finding the most changes wins.

* * *

GEO-DESIGN

PURPOSE: To allow students to display a degree of perception by having them choose pieces of a geometric figure to place with other figures.

GRADE LEVEL: 7th or 8th grade

TIME: 30-45 minutes

NUMBER: 3-6 players

METHOD OF CHECKING: Self-checking

MATERIALS:
1)   86 five-sided pieces that have segments of five different geometric designs printed on them. There should be three basic types of pieces:
   a) The pattern on this type of piece can be matched with one other like it to complete a single geometric design.

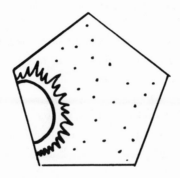

   b) The pattern on this type of piece consists of two segments, but they are of different geometric patterns. The geometric centers are at opposite sides.

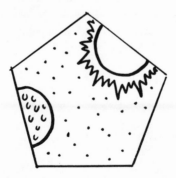

   c) The pattern on this type of piece consists of three segments with the geometric figures at opposite sides.

(Illustration appears on page 214)

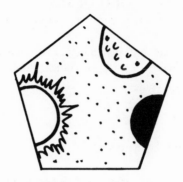

2)   1 die.

3)   Paper and pencil for scorekeeping.

4)   1 appropriately sized box for the materials.

PROCEDURE:

1)   The players gather around a table and are given the Geo-Design materials.

2)   Players roll the die to determine the order of play.

3)   The player rolling the highest score places all the pieces face down in the box and mixes them up.

4)   Each player draws 5 pieces from the box without letting the other players see them.

5)   The first player may place up to 3 pieces on the playing area, matching pattern edge to pattern edge. When the move is completed, he or she draws from the box the same number of pieces just played.

6)   Play passes to the left. Each player, in turn, adds pieces to the growing geometric design.

7)   At the end of each turn, a player must draw from the box the exact number of pieces played, so that there are always 5 pieces composing a hand.

8)   Note: Pieces may not be added to the design unless they match pieces already played; always matching along each edge.

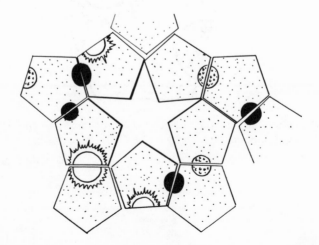

9)   A player may pass a turn only if new pieces cannot be added. At this time, the player may either choose to keep the pieces or exchange them all for new ones.

10) Plays in which patterns do not match along each edge that meets another piece are considered illegal.

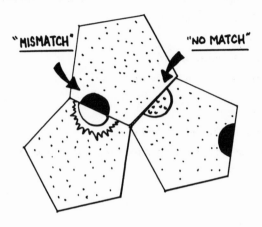

11) In addition, moves that leave an unfillable diamond shape space are illegal.

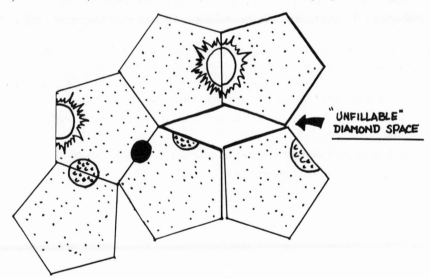

12) If a player makes an illegal play, the turn is lost and the pattern piece must be removed and played on his or her next turn.

13) One point is scored for each geometric pattern completed in a turn.

14) The game is over when all the pieces have been drawn and every player (including the player who made the last draw) has played one more time, or time runs out. Players are not penalized for segments left in their hands when the game ends.

15) The player with the highest total score is the winner.

* * *

COLLABORATE

PURPOSE: To allow students to combine humor and imagination while collaborating with others in designing a weird machine composed of mechanical parts that do nothing.

GRADE LEVEL: 7th or 8th grade

TIME: Two 45-minute periods

NUMBER: 8 players, 4 student judges

METHOD OF CHECKING: Student judges

MATERIALS:
1) Drawing supplies.

2) Catalogs, books on machinery, and so on.

3) 2 lists of possible components dry-mounted to a piece of colored posterboard. Some component examples are:

pulleys	gears
valves	switches
coils	

PROCEDURE:
1) The group is divided into two teams. The teams collaborate, using component lists, books on machinery, and catalogs to design and draw a weird machine that does nothing.

2) The time limit is 1 hour, 15 minutes, and all four team members must contribute to the drawing. (Each member might use a different colored pen.)

3) When the drawing is complete, a name and imaginary use for the machine is chosen. For example: The Gonkulater – used to produce educational jargon.

4) Four student judges are chosen and each team presents the weird machine to the judges.

5) Each judge rates each machine on a scale of 1-10 explaining reasons for the score.

6) The team with the most points wins.

* * *

PERCEPTION

PURPOSE: To promote skill in matching a description or word to an image.

GRADE LEVEL: 7th or 8th grade

TIME: 30 minutes

NUMBER: 4 students per pack of cards

METHOD OF CHECKING: Self-checking

MATERIALS:

1) 40 3x4-inch colored posterboard cards bearing descriptions and matching drawings. For example:

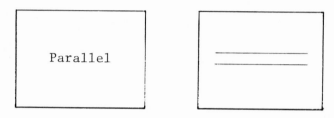

shadows	contour lines
silhouette	vertical
ellipse	balance
perspective	asymmetrical
subordinate	three dimensional
perpendicular	two dimensional
lower case letters	upper case letters
diagonal	repetition

2) Large manila envelope (10x13-inches) for the materials.

PROCEDURE:

1) Four students gather around a table and determine the order of play.

2) The first player becomes the dealer who shuffles the cards and places them face down on the table. The cards may be laid out in any pattern, but no two cards should touch.

3) Each player will want to remember the position of each card as it is turned up on the table, since this will help in building pairs.

4) The dealer starts the game by turning face up any two cards, one at a time. All players look at the two cards as they are turned up, but the two cards are not immediately picked up, just turned face up.

5) If the two cards are a pair, the dealer picks them up, keeps them, and turns up two more cards. A pair consists of the term and drawing. The dealer's turn continues as long as the two cards turned up form a pair.

6) If the two cards are not a pair, they are turned face down again and left in their original places. This ends the dealer's turn. (Cards are picked up only when they are a pair.)

(Procedures continue on page 218)

7) After the dealer's turn is over, the next player continues the game. Play continues as above.

8) The winner is the player who has accumulated the greatest number of correct pairs after all of the cards have been picked up from the table.

9) Each player scores one point for each pair held at the end of the game.

* * *

```
*****************************************************************
```
RIVAL
```
*****************************************************************
```

PURPOSE: To help students apply a word or descriptive phrase to a visual image empha-
    sizing such a description.

GRADE LEVEL: 7th or 8th grade

TIME: 35 minutes

NUMBER: 2 students per gameboard

METHOD OF CHECKING: Self-checking

MATERIALS:
1) 1 Rival gameboard made of 12x15-inch colored posterboard for every two students.

2) Visual images cut from postcards, calendars, catalogs, and so on. Images may be cut
   in different shapes that fit into a 2½x3-inch rectangle.

3) 12 3x5-inch index cards cut in half to measure 2½x3-inches bearing such words and
   descriptive phrases as:

sculpture	positive space
mosaic	profile of a person
portrait	bright, pure color
landscape	balance
still life	ceramics

4) Rubber cement or spray adhesive.

5) Large manila envelope (16x20-inches) for the materials.

PROCEDURE:
Preparation
1) Rule a piece of 12x15-inch colored posterboard into 24 sections 2½x3-inches to
   make a Rival gameboard.

2) Glue a visual image in each box. Number each box 1-24.

3) Write a word or descriptive phrase as suggested on one side of a 2½x3-inch card and
   put an easy arithmetic problem on the back of the card. For example: 17 - 8 = 9. The
   answer on the card should match the number of the box containing the example of
   the word or descriptive phrase.

Play
1) Players are given the Rival gameboard and cards and determine the order of play.

2) Cards are shuffled and placed above the board in a pile with the words and descriptive phrases face up.

3) The first player draws a card, reads the word or phrase, and places the card (word or
   phrase, face up) on the matching image.

4) The second player turns the card over and checks to see if the answer to the problem
   matches the number in the box.

5) If a match, the card is left in place. If not a match, the second player removes the
   card from the board, places it at the bottom of the pile and takes a turn. If a player

(Procedures continue on page 220)

draws a card and cannot match it, the card is placed at the bottom of the pile and the other player takes a turn.

6) Play continues in this fashion with players alternating turns.

7) The player that places the last card on the board wins.

* * *

```
*************************************************************
```
COLOR RELAY
```
*************************************************************
```

PURPOSE: To help students become more aware of the meanings of value, hue, tint, and shade, and to differentiate between variations of a color.

GRADE LEVEL: 7th or 8th grade

TIME: 30-45 minutes

NUMBER: 10 students

METHOD OF CHECKING: Self-checking/judge

MATERIALS:
1) 40 color chips from a paint store; 5 for each of 8 colors ranging from very light to very dark.

2) Black masking tape.

3) 8 letter-size envelopes.

4) Large manila envelope (12x15-inches) for the materials.

PROCEDURE:
Preparation
1) Bind the four outside edges of the color chips with black masking tape.

2) For self-checking, place an easy arithmetic problem on the back of the chip to indicate the correct position of that chip. For example: 3 - 1 = 2. This card would be correctly placed in the second position (*see* play 2).

3) Insert 5 chips of one color into each of the envelopes.

Play
1) The players are divided into two evenly matched teams, and each chooses a captain. The captains act as judges for the opposing teams.

2) The players form two lines (relay fashion) and sit on the floor facing a table. The captains are on either side of the table. The envelopes are placed in two piles on the table, as in the diagram below.

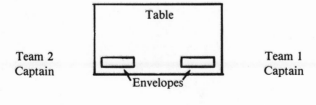

Team 1	Team 2
X	X
X	X
X	X
X	X

(Procedures continue on page 222)

3) The first player from each team goes to the table, picks an envelope, empties the chips on the table and arranges them in order from light to dark. When finished, the player notifies the judge who checks for correct arrangement of the chips.

4) If correctly arranged, the chips are placed in the envelope, which is given to the judge. If not correct, the player rearranges the chips, until the correct arrangement is found. After the envelope of chips is given to the judge, the player "tags" the next person in line and sits at the end of the line.

5) Play continues in this fashion.

6) The first team to finish the relay wins.

* * *

****
COLOR MATCH
****

PURPOSE: To promote skill at matching colors using projected light.

GRADE LEVEL: 7th or 8th grade

TIME: 40 minutes

NUMBER: 16 students to an entire class

METHOD OF CHECKING: Teacher

MATERIALS:

1) 50 color chips collected from a paint store put in a 10x13-inch envelope.

2) 1 medium-sized cardboard box; approximately 2x2-inches.

3) White sheet.

4) 3 dimmer switches.

5) 3 light sockets.

6) 3 bulbs (red, blue, green).

7) 2 wire caps.

8) 1 plug.

9) Tape.

10) Stopwatch, clock, or watch with a second hand.

PROCEDURE:

Preparation
See illustrated instructions on page 224.

Play

1) The group is divided into two teams. The teams form two lines (relay fashion) facing the Color Match contraption and determine order of play. The envelope containing color chips is placed next to the Color Match contraption.

2) A timekeeper is chosen and lights are dimmed.

3) The first player draws a color chip from the envelope and attempts to match the color of the chip with the color emanating from the Color Match contraption within three minutes. Dimmer switches can be turned to provide less or more color intensity.

4) If the player does match the chip within the time limit, the team is given a point, and the chip is placed in a discard pile. If no match is achieved, no points are scored, the chip is returned to the envelope, and the other team takes a turn.

5) The teacher determines whether or not a match is achieved.

6) Play continues with teams alternating turns.

7) The team with the most points wins.

Color Match Contraption

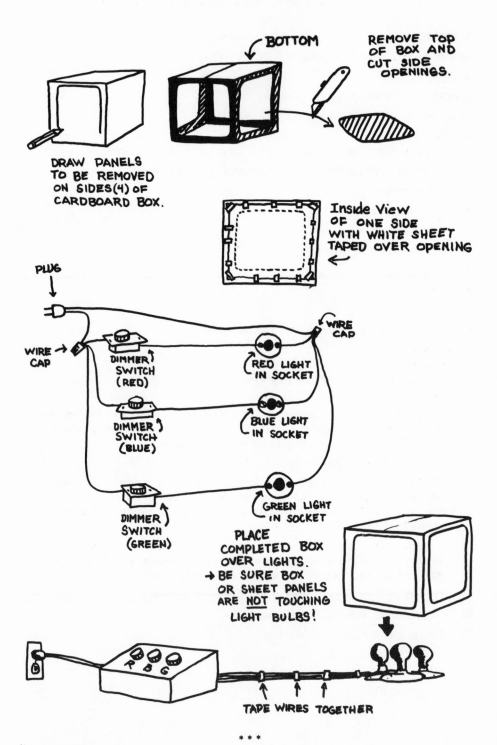

BOTTOM

REMOVE TOP OF BOX AND CUT SIDE OPENINGS.

DRAW PANELS TO BE REMOVED ON SIDES (4) OF CARDBOARD BOX.

Inside View OF ONE SIDE WITH WHITE SHEET TAPED OVER OPENING

PLUG

WIRE CAP

WIRE CAP

DIMMER SWITCH (RED)

RED LIGHT IN SOCKET

DIMMER SWITCH (BLUE)

BLUE LIGHT IN SOCKET

DIMMER SWITCH (GREEN)

GREEN LIGHT IN SOCKET

PLACE COMPLETED BOX OVER LIGHTS.
→ BE SURE BOX OR SHEET PANELS ARE <u>NOT</u> TOUCHING LIGHT BULBS!

R B G

TAPE WIRES TOGETHER

* * *

```
************************************************************
```
TONE RELAY
```
************************************************************
```

PURPOSE: To help students recognize the number of tones that exist in a black-and-white picture.

GRADE LEVEL: 7th or 8th grade

TIME: 30 minutes

NUMBER: 16 students

METHOD OF CHECKING: Teacher and/or answer sheet

MATERIALS:
1) 2 slide projectors.

2) 2 pieces of white butcher paper approximately 4x4-feet, 1 chalkboard.

3) 2 black and white slides of students or teachers.

4) 2 magic markers.

5) Answer sheet—drawing of the slides with the different tones outlined in pen.

PROCEDURE:
Preparation
1) Butcher paper is taped on the chalkboard.

2) The two slide projectors are positioned and the slides are projected onto the butcher paper.

3) Note: A magazine picture may be used to make a transparency so that overhead projectors can be used.

Play
1) The group is divided into two teams. Each team sits in a line facing a piece of butcher paper on which the slide is projected.

2) The first player of each team is given a magic marker, goes to the butcher paper, outlines a tonal area of the projected slide, gives the magic marker to the next player, and sits down at the end of the line.

3) Play continues until each player has had two turns.

4) The first team to finish wins.

* * *

TEXTURE TOUCH

PURPOSE: To train students to differentiate among various textures.

GRADE LEVEL: 7th or 8th grade

TIME: 45 minutes

NUMBER: 15 students

METHOD OF CHECKING: Self-checking as answers are given during a discussion period

MATERIALS:

1) 2 cardboard boxes approximately 12x16x11½-inches with 4 cardboard dividers placed inside each box. Boxes are inverted, openings are cut in the four sides, and the sections are numbered.

2) 8 types of materials of different textures. For example:

salt	steel wool
wet noodles in a plastic bag	soap powder
sponge	wig
brick	dried cactus

3) Paper and pencil for each student.

PROCEDURE:

1) Students number a piece of paper from 1-8 and take turns feeling inside each section of the boxes.

2) The students attempt to identify the materials by feeling the texture only and list the name of the material on the paper.

3) When finished, each student chooses one texture to illustrate.

4) During a discussion period, after the students have completed a list and illustration, each person checks his or her paper.

5) Each student receives 10 points for a completed texture illustration and 1 point for each object correctly guessed.

6) The student with the most points wins.

* * *

MASTERWORKS MEMORY

PURPOSE: To familiarize students with paintings and sculptures from many countries.

GRADE LEVEL: 7th or 8th grade

TIME: 25 minutes

NUMBER: 2 students per pack of cards

METHOD OF CHECKING: Self-checking

MATERIALS:

1) A "Masterworks" stamp collecting kit available from the U.S. Post Office featuring paintings and sculptures from many lands.

2) 50 3x4-inch colored posterboard cards. 25 "Masterworks" stamps are mounted on half of the cards, and the cards are numbered 1-25 in the lower right-hand corner. The remaining cards are also numbered 1-25 and the artists' names and/or countries are placed on the cards.

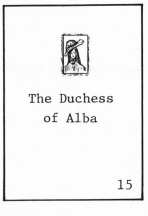

3) Large manila envelope (12x15-inches) for the materials.

PROCEDURE:

1) Two students sit at a table and determine the order of play.

2) The first player becomes the dealer, shuffles the cards, and places them face down on the table. The cards may be laid out in any pattern, but no two cards should touch.

3) Each player will want to remember the position of each card as it is turned up on the table, since this will help in building pairs.

4) The dealer starts the game by turning face up any two cards, one at a time. Both players look at the two cards as they are turned up, but the two cards are not immediately picked up, just turned face up.

5) If the two cards are a pair, the dealer picks them up, keeps them, and turns up two more cards. The dealer's turn continues as long as the cards turned up compose a

(Procedures continue on page 228)

pair. A pair consists of the "Masterworks" stamp and the artist and/or country. For example: The Duchess of Alba — Francisco Goya/Spain.

6) If the two cards are not a pair, they are turned face down again and left in their original places. This ends the dealer's turn. (Cards are picked up only when they form a pair.)

7) After the dealer's turn is over, the next player continues the game. Play continues as above.

8) The winner is the player who has accumulated the greatest number of correct pairs after all of the cards have been picked up from the table.

* * *

****

ART COLLECTOR

****

PURPOSE: To familiarize students with individual artists and with each artist's works.

GRADE LEVEL: 7th or 8th grade

TIME: 30 minutes

NUMBER: 3-6 students per pack of cards

METHOD OF CHECKING: Self-checking

MATERIALS:

1)   13 "sets" of 4 (total 52) cards approximately 2½x3½-inches bearing works by an artist and the artist's name. A "set" is 4 different works by one artist. (Note: Small reproductions of great art may be gleaned from museum postcards, catalogs, and postage stamps, as well as from commercial suppliers.)

2)   Large manila envelope (12x15-inches) for the materials.

PROCEDURE:

1)   The cards are dealt, one at a time, until all cards are given out. The number of cards received is not important; some players may have more cards than others.

2)   The player to the left of the dealer begins by calling on another player and requesting a card, e.g., "Sue, give me a painting by Matisse."

3)   If the player addressed has the card specified, the card must be given to the first player. As long as the first player is successful in getting cards, he or she continues taking turns. When unsuccessful, the turn passes to the left.

4)   When a player gets all four cards of one artist, the "set" is shown to all players and placed on the table.

5)   The player collecting the most "sets" wins the game.

* * *

PORTRAIT PUZZLERS

PURPOSE: To allow students to have fun while becoming acquainted with famous artists and works of art.

GRADE LEVEL: 7th or 8th grade

TIME: 30 minutes

NUMBER: 1 student per puzzle

METHOD OF CHECKING: Self-checking

MATERIALS:

1) Poster-size reproductions of famous works of art.

2) Rubber cement or spray adhesive.

3) Posterboard.

4) Pencils and paper.

5) Large manila envelope (10x13-inches) for the materials.

PROCEDURE:

Preparation

1) Mount reproductions on posterboard and laminate.

2) Cut into over-sized jigsaw puzzle pieces.

3) Store puzzle pieces in manila envelopes.

Play

1) Two players are each given a Portrait Puzzle.

2) The players race to put the puzzles together.

3) When the puzzle is completed, the player must identify the work, identify the artist, and write two interesting facts about the artist using art reference books or materials.

4) The first player to complete all the tasks wins.

* * *

```
****************************************************************
```
CELEBRITIES
```
****************************************************************
```

PURPOSE: To provide exposure to capsule biographies of some American artists, illustrators, and cartoonists.

GRADE LEVEL: 7th or 8th grade

TIME: 40 minutes

NUMBER: 2 students per gameboard

METHOD OF CHECKING: Self-checking

MATERIALS:
1)   1 Celebrities gameboard made from 14x22-inch posterboard.

2)   1 die.

3)   2 markers per gameboard.

4)   20 3x4-inch colored posterboard celebrity cards bearing names of American artists, illustrators, and cartoonists. Some examples are:

Abbey, Edwin	De Paola, Tomie
Akeley, Carl	Geisel, Theodor
Albers, Josef	Glackens, William
Albright, Ivan	Schulz, Charles
Davies, Arthur	Seegar, Elzie

5)   10 3x4-inch colored posterboard star cards bearing directions such as:

Lose 1 turn	Move ahead 1 space
Go back 3 spaces	Move ahead 2 spaces

(Materials list continues on page 232)

6) *Webster's American Biographies* (Springfield, MA: G&C Merriam, 1975).

7) Stopwatch, clock, or watch with a second hand.

8) Large manila envelope (16x20-inches) for the materials.

PROCEDURE:

1) Players are given a Celebrities gameboard and related materials.

2) Cards are shuffled and placed face down in a pile in the appropriate space on the board.

3) Markers are placed on start and players determine the order of play.

4) The first player begins by drawing a card and looking the person up in *Webster's American Biographies*. If the biography is found within 1 minute, the player reads it aloud, places the card at the bottom of the pile, rolls the die, and moves the number of spaces indicated. If time runs out, no move is made and player 2 takes a turn.

5) Play continues with players alternating turns. When a player lands on a space marked with a star, a star card is drawn and directions must be followed.

6) The first player to reach "End" wins.

* * *

```
*************************************************************
```
ISMS
```
*************************************************************
```

PURPOSE: To familiarize students with schools of art.

GRADE LEVEL: 7th and 8th grade

TIME: 45 minutes

NUMBER: 8 students

METHOD OF CHECKING: Answer key

MATERIALS:
1) A wide variety of slides of art works representing different schools with enough slides to form 2 sets (40-80 slides). Each slide should be numbered for ease in checking.

2) 1 title slide for each of the "Isms" used:

Abstract expressionism	Classicism
Cubism	Dadaism
Expressionism	Fauvism
Futurism	Impressionism
Neo-impressionism	Pointillism
Post Impressionism	Realism
Romanticism	Surrealism

3) 2 slide trays.

4) 2 sorting trays or 2 slide projectors.

5) Answer key example:

1, 6, 12 cubism (to be kept by the media specialist or teacher until teams complete sorting.)

PROCEDURE:
1) The students are divided into two teams.

2) Each team is given a slide tray and a number of slides (20-40) including title slides.

3) The slides are to be grouped behind a title slide according to schools of art within 30 minutes. Art reference materials may be consulted if necessary.

4) When finished, the teams get the answer key and check for correct grouping of slides.

5) Each team receives a point for a slide placed within the correct school.

6) The team with the most points wins.

7) Note: Art reproductions may be used if slides are not available.

* * *

APPENDIX

PROGRESSIONS OF IMC SKILLS

Alphabetical Order

Sample Objective: The student will be able to apply knowledge of alphabetical order by demonstrating an ability to locate IMC materials successfully 90% of the time, as measured by teacher observation.

Concept	Grade Introduced/Reinforced K 1 2 3 4 5 6 7 8 9
Arrange simple words alphabetically by initial letter	X X X X X X X X X X
Arrange through 2nd and 3rd letters	X X X X X X X X X
Arrange through 4th thru 7th letters	X X X X X X X
Arrange by word	X X X X X X X
Alphabetize by author	X X X X X X X
Alphabetize by title	X X X X X X

Parts of a Book and IMC Vocabulary

Sample Objective: The student will demonstrate with 80% accuracy the ability to apply a knowledge of the parts of a book and IMC terminology by effective use of materials 90% of the time, as measured by teacher observation.

Concept	Grade Introduced/Reinforced K 1 2 3 4 5 6 7 8 9
Title, author	X X X X X X X X X X
Call number, illustration, page number	X X X X X X X X X X
Title page, table of contents, body of book, glossary, spine, cover, jacket	X X X X X X X
Copyright date and its meaning	X X X X X X X
Foreword, preface, appendix, index, flyleaf, frontispiece, introduction	X X X X X X
Bibliography	X X X X X X
Dedication, acknowledgments, editor, edition	X X X X X
Publishing company, place of printing	X X X X X
List of illustrations, translator	X X X X X
Author synopsis	X X X X X
Prologue, epilogue	X X X X
Index of authors, index of titles	X X X X
Index of first lines, index abbreviations	X X X X
Footnotes	X X X X

Card Catalog

Sample Objective: The student, by applying knowledge of the card catalog, will be able to locate information by author, title, and subject 90% of the time, as measured by teacher observation.

Concept	K	1	2	3	4	5	6	7	8	9
Location, definition, purpose, arrangement of trays	X	X	X	X	X	X	X			
Identify the three kinds of cards used by distinguishing the different types of entries as they appear on the first line of the catalog card	X	X	X	X	X	X	X			
Locate books by author, title, and subject	X	X	X	X	X	X	X			
Use of outside and inside guides in the tray	X	X	X	X	X	X	X			
Locate the call number on the card, and use this information to find a book on the shelves	X	X	X	X	X	X	X	X		
Type of cards for various kinds of media			X	X	X	X	X	X		
Locate the nonprint media call number on the card and use this information to find the item in the IMC				X	X	X	X	X	X	

Grade Introduced/Reinforced

Skills Chart
Location of Books and the Dewey Decimal Classification System

Sample Objective: The student will apply knowledge of the arrangement of books in the IMC by being able independently to locate needed items 90% of the time, as measured by teacher observation.

Concept	K	1	2	3	4	5	6	7	8	9
Easy and picture books	X	X	X	X	X	X	X	X	X	X
Meaning of call numbers on books		X	X	X	X	X	X	X	X	X
Use of call numbers in finding books on shelves		X	X	X	X	X	X	X	X	X
Fiction and nonfiction location			X	X	X	X	X	X	X	X
Myths and legends, fairy tales, poetry, science, geography, space, music, sports, history, reference					X	X	X	X	X	X
Individual and collective biography					X	X	X	X	X	X
Ten main divisions of the Dewey Decimal Classification System					X	X	X	X	X	X
Arrangement of books within the Dewey Decimal Classification System						X	X	X	X	X

Grade Introduced/Reinforced

Dictionary Reference Skills

Sample Objective: The student, given the need to define or spell a word, will be able to apply a knowledge of dictionary skills to locate the needed word 90% of the time, as measured by teacher observation.

Concept	Grade Introduced/Reinforced										
	K	1	2	3	4	5	6	7	8	9
Alphabetical arrangement of the dictionary	X	X	X	X	X	X	X	X	X	
Division of dictionary into front, middle, back parts			X	X	X	X	X	X	X	
Locate words in the dictionary by using guide words			X	X	X	X	X	X	X	
Selective use of various meanings for words				X	X	X	X	X	X	
Antonyms, homonyms, synonyms, syllabication, thumb index					X	X	X	X	X	
Unabridged and special dictionaries					X	X	X	X	X	
Locate material in special dictionaries					X	X	X	X	X	
Find abbreviations and parts of speech					X	X	X	X	X	
Locate hyphenated words, special information, word history, prefixes, suffixes, pictures, and illustrations					X	X	X	X	X	
Special sections at beginning and end of dictionaries						X	X	X	X	

Encyclopedia Reference Skills

Sample Objective: The student will be able to show the ability to use an encyclopedia by successfully locating information 80% of the time without teacher assistance, as measured by teacher observation.

Concept	Grade Introduced/Reinforced										
	K	1	2	3	4	5	6	7	8	9
Location and purpose of encyclopedias in the library				X	X	X	X	X	X	X
Arrangement and types of information found in encyclopedias				X	X	X	X	X	X	X
Difference between encyclopedias and dictionaries				X	X	X	X	X	X	X
Use of the index in an encyclopedia					X	X	X	X	X	X
Ability to obtain information from encyclopedias					X	X	X	X	X	X
Use of cross-reference and related subject references						X	X	X	X	X
Organize facts for specific purposes through the use of the encyclopedia							X	X	X	X
Know the names and scope of several important encyclopedias								X	X	X
Special subject encyclopedias								X	X	X
Know the differences in treatment of individual subjects by the encyclopedias									X	X

Special Reference Materials

Sample Objective: The student will be able to select and use appropriate reference materials 50% of the time with minimal teacher assistance, as measured by teacher observation.

Concept	Grade Introduced/Reinforced K 1 2 3 4 5 6 7 8 9
Atlases, Maps, and globes	X X X X X X X X
Special references:	
almanacs	X X X X X X
biographical dictionaries	X X X X X
Junior Book of Authors, More Junior	
Authors, Children's Literature Review,	
and *Something about the Author*	X X X X X
Vertical files:	
pictures and pamphlet materials,	
periodical articles, newspaper clippings	X X X X X
Selection of appropriate reference tool	X X X X X
Special indexes:	
National Geographic Index, 1947-1976;	
Abridged Readers' Guide to Periodical	
Literature; Poetry Index; Short Story	
Index; Plays Index; and so on	X X X X
Effective use of reference tools	X X X X

Care of Media

Sample Objective: The student will display a sense of the value of media by demonstrating care for print and nonprint materials 90% of the time, as measured by teacher observation.

Concept	Grade Introduced/Reinforced K 1 2 3 4 5 6 7 8 9
Handle books and periodicals carefully	
avoid dropping, avoid damage, safety,	
bookmarks, cleanliness	X X X X X X X X X X
correct shelving	X X X X X X X X X
Handle nonprint materials so as to prevent harm	
cleanliness, safety	X X X X X X X X X X
proper insertion of material into machines	X X X X X X X X

Kinds of Media

Sample Objective: The student will display an ability to identify and select suitable print and nonprint material for that student's information and recreational reading needs 80% of the time, as measured by teacher observation.

Concept	Grade Introduced/Reinforced K 1 2 3 4 5 6 7 8 9
Identify and select print materials	
books	X X X X X X X X X X
periodicals, maps	X X X X X X X X
vertical file material	X X X X X X
Identify and select nonprint materials	
models, realia	X X X X X X X X X X
audio flashcards, Viewmaster®	X X X X X X X X
study prints, 8mm film loops, cassettes	X X X X X X X X
slides, kits, transparencies, filmstrips,	
phonodiscs	X X X X X X X
films, reel-to-reel tapes	X X X X X X
video tapes	X X X X
microforms	X X X

Nonprint Media Reference Skills

Sample Objective: The student will be able to show the ability to use nonprint media for reference by successfully locating information 75% of the time without teacher assistance, as measured by teacher observation.

Concept	Grade Introduced/Reinforced K 1 2 3 4 5 6 7 8 9
Ability to obtain information from nonprint media	X X X X X X
Organize facts for specific purposes through the use of nonprint media	X X X X X

Use of Equipment

Sample Objective: The student will demonstrate proficiency in using equipment 85% of the time without teacher assistance, as measured by teacher observation.

Concept	K	1	2	3	4	5	6	7	8	9
Language Master®, headset	X	X	X	X	X	X	X	X	X	X
Cassette recorder, record player, filmstrip viewer, listening center, television, Viewmaster®, audio flash card reader		X	X	X	X	X	X	X	X	X
8mm loop projector, previewer		X	X	X	X	X	X	X	X	X
Overhead projector, still camera				X	X	X	X	X	X	X
Filmstrip projector/viewer, Dukane projector, opaque projector					X	X	X	X	X	X
16mm projector, slide projector/viewer						X	X	X	X	X
Reel-to-reel tape recorder, video tape recorder							X	X	X	X
Laminator/dry mounter, microform readers, video/movie camera								X	X	X
Microform reader/printers										X

Production Skills

Sample Objective: The student will master educational media production skills 80% of the time and thus be able to contribute further to the total educational process, as measured by teacher observation.

Concept	K	1	2	3	4	5	6	7	8	9
Media photography:										
general photography—pictures				X	X	X	X	X	X	X
general photography—slides					X	X	X	X	X	X
use of copy stands						X	X	X	X	X
synchronizing sight and sound								X	X	X
8mm film										X
Script writing:										
storyboarding								X	X	X
editing, media selection										X
Graphics:										
transparencies				X	X	X	X	X	X	X
laminating, dry-mounting								X	X	X
layout										X
Recording:										
audio tape		X	X	X	X	X	X	X	X	X
video tape								X	X	X

Report and Research Projects

Sample Objective: The student will demonstrate knowledge of appropriate methods of preparing oral and written reports and research projects 90% of the time, as measured by teacher observation.

Concept	K	1	2	3	4	5	6	7	8	9
Grade Introduced/Reinforced										
Organizing time				X	X	X	X	X	X	X
Searching for information:										
finding information pertaining to the topic				X	X	X	X	X	X	X
taking research notes				X	X	X	X	X	X	X
preparing and using a working bibliography; selecting and limiting a topic							X	X	X	X
Organizing techniques:										
theory of and respect for copyright plagiarism, quotations					X	X	X	X	X	X
using logical sequence					X	X	X	X	X	X
writing and rewriting					X	X	X	X	X	X
supporting a main idea							X	X	X	X
collating and synthesizing material from two or more sources							X	X	X	X
Presentation techniques:										
oral, audiovisual, written			X	X	X	X	X	X	X	X
making an outline						X	X	X	X	X
making notecards, bibliographies							X	X	X	X
using footnotes								X	X	X
format of text									X	X

ABOUT THE AUTHORS

JEANNE E. WIECKERT, 1939- . Born in Chicago, she holds degrees from the University of Northern Illinois (Education) and the University of Northern Colorado (Curriculum and Instruction with emphasis in International Education). A former Chicago Public School teacher (K-8), she is now a Media Specialist (K-6) with the Denver Public Schools. Mrs. Wieckert has presented several workshops in the Colorado region as a result of her interest in affective education and as a result of her recent media skills books. A current series of workshops presented by Mrs. Wieckert for the Nebraska Media Association, the Educational Service Unit #3 in cooperation with the Millard School District, and Creighton University included "Media Skills Gaming: Techniques and Time Savers" and "Learning Centers: Organization, Preparation, Implementation." She has recently received a grant to do further study in the area of teaching through gaming and is also involved in programming games from *Basic Media Skills through Games* (Libraries Unlimited, 1979) for computer use. She is also co-authoring a second skills book for the junior high level. She is a member of the American Library Association (ALA), American Association of School Librarians (AASL), and the Colorado Educational Media Association (CEMA). Mrs. Wieckert lives in Boulder County, Colorado with her husband and two children.

IRENE W. BELL, 1944- . Born in New York City, she holds degrees from the State University College at Potsdam, New York (B.A. in Social Sciences), the University of Massachusetts (M.A. in American History), and the University of Denver (M.A. in Librarianship). A former junior high school history teacher with the Ipswich, Massachusetts Public Schools, she is now a Media Specialist (K-6) with the Denver Public Schools. Ms. Bell has currently completed a series of workshops for the State Department of education (Wyoming) on "Gaming: An Alternative to Teaching Library Skills" and was involved with the Association for Educational Communications & Technology (AECT) presenting "Gaming through Media" and with the Colorado Educational Media Association (CEMA) presenting "Gaming in the Media Center." She is the co-author of *Basic Media Skills through Games* (Libraries Unlimited, 1979) and *Basic Classroom Skills through Games* (Libraries Unlimited, 1980), and is engaged in writing a second skills book for the junior high level. She is a member of the American Library Association (ALA), the American Association of School Librarians (AASL), and the Colorado Educational Media Association (CEMA). At present, Ms. Bell resides in Littleton, Colorado with her husband and two cats.

ABOUT THE ILLUSTRATOR

JAY CONLEY, 1948- . Born in Baird, Texas, he holds a degree from the University of Denver (B.F.A. in Fine Arts) and is currently working on an M.A. in Media at the University of Northern Colorado. Before becoming an art instructor at Brighton High School, Brighton, Colorado, Mr. Conley was a commercial artist. His most recent work for Libraries Unlimited was *Basic Classroom Skills through Games*. Presently Mr. Conley resides in Northglenn, Colorado with his wife, son, and daughter.

INDEX OF GAME TITLES

SELECTION INDEXES

This index takes into account three major categories: Method of Checking; Number of Students; and Type of Game.

III. TYPE OF GAME

Card Games:

Gameboard & Cards: